HERE WITH ME

A JOURNEY OF HOPE

CHRISTINA PICKETT

WESTBOW
PRESS®
A DIVISION OF THOMAS NELSON
& ZONDERVAN

WestBow Press books may be ordered through booksellers or by contacting:

WestBow Press
A Division of Thomas Nelson & Zondervan
1663 Liberty Drive
Bloomington, IN 47403
www.westbowpress.com
844-714-3454

ISBN: 978-1-9736-9961-3 (sc)
ISBN: 978-1-9736-9962-0 (hc)
ISBN: 978-1-9736-9960-6 (e)

Library of Congress Control Number: 2023909844

Print information available on the last page.

WestBow Press rev. date: 06/07/2023

To my nephews and nieces, Donavan, Joshué, Deadria, and Victavia. I pray that my life reflects resilient hope in the hands of a loving God. I pray that you can see past my failures and observe the true reflection of my heart that longs to know my Savior more each day. May your lives far exceed all that you have ever hoped or imagined.

Seek the LORD to learn of those things. May Jesus receive all the glory. Amen.

CONTENTS

PREFACE

As she lay there in bed, she reflected on the deadness of her soul. There was no excitement in store for her during this new day, just daily chores and work. Business as usual. As she forced herself out of bed, the dread of the mundane weighed heavily upon her, leaving little strength to get started with the day. She shuffled into the washroom and found more displeasure at the reflection she saw as she gazed at herself in the mirrored reflection. Releasing an all too familiar sigh, she placed the basic blue and white patterned headscarf over her hair and dressed in attire suitable for society.

As she journeyed through her day, she noticed an uncommon commotion taking place in the market. She discreetly positioned herself closer to the clusters of people to hear what all the excitement was about. Some of the people raved about personal experiences and others went on about His great wisdom. She listened as one woman seemed to weep with great joy as she shared with her companions how this same Man touched her and healed her body. There was another gentleman overjoyed at how this same Man had forgiven him of all that he had done and how he has a greater hope in life because of this wonderful Stranger.

Hope suddenly filled her like never before. She was a woman of great sin in the eyes of most because of how public her sins were. She felt a rush of excitement as her mind considered the possibility of freedom from her poor choices, healing in her soul, and acceptance by someone as honored as this esteemed Man seemed to be.

She dropped the plans she had made for herself for the remainder of the day and learned where the Man would be having dinner. As she went to that place, she found herself filled with belief of His acceptance and immense hope of finally becoming complete in a way that her sins were not able to satisfy.

As she lingered near the threshold of the door, she began to question her actions. *What will they think of me? What will they do to me? Will I be thrown out and discarded as trash?* Their stares already spoke volumes of their disgust as she decided to move toward the honored guest. With every step she took, fear started to grip every part of her being. It caused her legs to feel as though twenty pounds of weight had been added to each of them. Her heart started to race uncontrollably, and her nerves had become obvious to all who looked upon her. To help control her trembling, she clung with both her hands to the precious vial she wore around her neck. The vial was very precious and dear to her, so this action brought her great comfort as she drew nearer to this honored guest. Her mind became flooded with all the sins she had committed and those that were committed toward her. Her heart was deeply pained at the remembrance of all the opportunities lost, the abandonment of friends and family members, and the public rejection of her by society. The woman's heart was wounded and broken indeed.

With her head hung low and finally standing at the feet of the guest, all her thoughts slowly evaporated from her mind and were replaced by deep gratitude. Words would not part from her lips, yet her emotions were becoming revealed to all as she wept. As stillness filled the room and with the accusing voices in her head now silenced, nothing mattered to her. Now standing so close in His presence, all her pain and guilt seemed to melt away. The ache in her heart was replaced with tenderness as she embraced the sense of love and compassion coming from the Stranger. Overwhelmed by an unfamiliar expression of joy, rich rivers of tears began to stream down her face and wash over the feet of this wonderful Man. Her next instinct drove her to bow, kiss, and wipe her tears off the feet of this precious Man who had revealed to her, her true value and worth. It was as if this Man knew every secret thought. And while many of those thoughts became actions, she felt accepted by Him without reservations.

As she wiped His feet with her hair, she desperately longed for a way to more lavishly express her gratitude. She then remembered the vial of perfumed oil on the chain around her neck. *Is He the reason I spent all I had to purchase this oil and have kept it so close to my heart?* She was filled with great delight thinking of the possibility. Without considering more of the matter, she broke it open and anointed His feet with the perfumed oil.

A woman in that town who lived a sinful life learned that Jesus was eating at the Pharisee's house, so she came there with an alabaster jar of perfume. As she stood behind him at his feet weeping, she began to wet his feet with her tears. Then she wiped them with her hair, kissed them and poured perfume on them.

When the Pharisee who had invited him saw this, he said to himself, "If this man were a prophet, he would know who is touching him and what kind of woman she is—that she is a sinner."

Then Jesus said to her, "Your sins are forgiven."

Jesus said to the woman, "Your faith has saved you; go in peace." (Luke 7:37–39, 48, 50 NIV; read verses 36–50 for the full context)

I cannot say if this is what was going on in her mind during one unique day of this woman. No one can. The Bible does not clearly state what the sins of this woman were; they can only be imagined. I can only infer that her sins were great because the rich Pharisees were aware of them. That could lead one to further speculate: If they were aware of who she was and the type of sins she committed, I would question if they were also committing those sins with her. Gossip or speculation? You decide. The Bible identifies her as a woman who lived a sinful life, and the Bible also says she was forgiven. And this one special day and special encounter with Jesus, the wonderful Savior, changed her life and the lives of many others forever. I heard Eric Souza of Cornerstone Chapel in Leesburg, Virginia, say something that pretty much sums up this scene:

"When Simon looked at her, he saw a dirty woman. But when Jesus looked at her, He saw a devoted woman. When Simon looked at her, he saw her as a disgrace; Jesus looked at her, and He saw her as a disciple. Simon saw her reputation, her sin; Jesus saw her repentance. Simon, when he looked at her, was filled with contempt. Jesus was filled with compassion. And lastly, Simon saw her as she was because of what she had done. Jesus saw her as she is because of what she's doing.

If you are not a believer, do not ever let the judgmental glares of legalistic people keep you from coming to Christ. I promise you He sees you very differently than they do."

A Defining Moment

Which statement holds the most truth for you? Circle true or false.

1. We judge because we are often judged by others. True or False
2. We judge because we have been harshly judged by others. True or False
3. Which one (question 1 or 2) do you find yourself most guilty of and why?

I am currently living in an area of town where the class of people is much greater than I could afford outside the blessing of God. Naturally, we tend to shop in the areas nearest our home and do all our business within a five-to-ten-mile radius. I went to vote, and the gentleman who greeted me had a look of surprise on his face when I verified with him that my voting district was in that zone. There was another incident when I took my niece and sister on a girls' day out. I booked appointments for pedicures across the street from my home. They were soliciting new customers, which is typical because they were a new establishment, and I offered some suggestions based on how I had seen advertisements within my apartment complex. The lady said to me, "No, in your neighborhood."

I smiled and politely said, "This is my neighborhood." She had a look of shock on her face.

Why do we judge each other based on appearances? True, some people can carry themselves suspiciously and will cause you to discretely clutch your pocketbook. But it is heartbreaking when you are among your own, other believers, and feel the vibes of discrimination in the environment of a Bible study. That happened to me recently as well.

But take great comfort. The Lord sees the judgment and legalism being shown toward you. He is aware of the hearts and thoughts directed toward you. Are you that prostitute or have you purchased one? Are you a drug addict or the one selling the drugs? Are you a thief stealing from your job, other businesses, or family members? Are you the one whose mind is constantly filled with lustful desires and allow yourself to be satisfied with porn? Do you rage with anger and cause a slow, agonizing death of the ones who love you by physically or verbally abusing them almost daily with your acts of cruelty?

I believe all these sins mentioned, and many others not listed, greatly displeases the heart of the Father. But I believe what displeases Him more is when we practice a sin but find fault in our brothers or sisters in the faith who commit the same types of sin as we do. Better yet, we find fault with them for the same or similar sins that He has delivered us from, yet we yield in showing grace to them for their moments of weakness. I have often been found guilty of this offense, and I must often ask for forgiveness.

> Why do you see the speck that is in your brother's eye, but do not notice the log that is in your own eye? Or how can you say to your brother, "Let me take the speck out of your eye," when there is the log in your own eye? You hypocrite, first take the log out of your own eye, and then you will see clearly to take the speck out of your brother's eye. (Matthew 7:3–5 ESV)

We will revisit this thought a little later in this book.

INTRODUCTION

Shortly after writing my first book, *A Shadow of Death*, a few people expressed interest in more details about what led to the major transitions of my past. On discussing the various obstacles and contrasting them with their present struggles, I started to notice many patterns of their trials matched perfectly with pockets of my own difficulties in the past.

Because of my past obstacles, I have gained more understanding of how God can take many of our challenging moments and use them for something of great benefit. What is good and how can it be defined? In all fairness, it's impossible to compare anything tangible in our lives today to the type of good that equates to God. The tangibles in our lives tend to devalue over time. For example, you find a good used car today. But tomorrow it has lost value, yet you've only driven it a few miles. After you build a new home, start a new business, and so on, the value of it changes daily. When I speak of good in reference to God, great understanding can be gained by observing His attributes. His attributes do not lose value over time. Yet, they remain consistent, unwavering, and unchanging. Let's look at a few of them and contrast them with ours.

- Humankind is often guided by emotions, circumstances, or learned habits; God does not change (Psalm 102:27; Malachi 3:6; James 1:17).
- We are dependent on creation (a home, food, clothing, and so on), but He is independent of any needs from His creation (Acts 17:24–25) because He created all things (Revelation 4:11).
- Humans are limited in understanding, but God sees and knows all things (Psalm 139:7–10; Matthew 10:30; Psalm 139:16).

O Lord, how manifold are your works! In wisdom have
you made them all; the earth is full of your creatures.
(Psalm 104:24 ESV)

- God is good; there is no darkness (hate) found in Him (Luke
  18:19; 1 John 1:5). Can we say the same of ourselves?
- He is full of compassion, shows grace and is patient, long-
  suffering, and faithful (Exodus 34:6). Do we struggle with
  showing compassion and grace or being long-suffering, patient,
  and impartial?

These attributes only scratch the surface of how He is described
throughout the scriptures. God is full of goodness simply because He is
good. He invites us to sit with Him daily to teach His goodness to us so
that we may share it with others. Daily, He leads us toward the truth of
His salvation. If we allow Him to, He will take all the painful moments
of our lives and heal them with hope and understanding.

Through prayer, fellowship, and daily devotion, I have learned many of
His truths and gained much understanding of His will for my life. I have
also learned how much He is here with me and always has been throughout
my very personal journey of hope in Christ Jesus, my Lord. God desires
intimacy with each of us. He desires to show us great and mighty things
if we seek Him with all our hearts.

Call to Me, and I will answer you, and show you great
and mighty things, which you do not know. (Jeremiah
33:3 NKJV)

What about you? Do you believe God is good? Do you doubt there is
a God? Do you question your intimacy with God? Are you aware of God's
love for you? Have you experienced God's love or seen His love on display
in someone else's life? Do you believe that God speaks to you and desires
to guide you through life daily? If you confess to being a Christian, do you
trust God with your life, or are you afraid to release that control to Him?

My friend, if we are honest, we all have had these questions at some
point. Would you take a journey with me as I share my pain, shame, and

fears in the hope that you can further your path in Christ's freedom? Would you sit a while with me as I sift through the ashes of my life and show you how God is making it beautiful? I know that my Redeemer lives, and my desire is for you to know this truth as well.

As I share my journey of hope with you and shine the light of God's Word on many of the dark moments in my life, my hope is this book will help you see God in the details of yours. God is our refuge and strength, always ready to help in times of trouble (Psalm 46:1 NLT). His desire for one is His desire for all.

> For there is no respect of persons with God. (Romans 2:11 KJV)

As I share my journey with you, a series of questions will be asked throughout and at the end of each section. The purpose of each question is to lead you into a deep search within your heart to allow God to uproot any hindrances keeping you from true freedom in Him. I challenge you to be transparent with your answers and vulnerable in prayer to God the Father. I pray that you accept the challenge to allow Him to continue to sanctify your soul. And I pray for your strength throughout your journey. May the Holy Spirit teach and instruct you in all things, and may your heart yearn to pick up your cross daily and follow Jesus. In His name, Jesus Christ the Lord, Amen.

REJECTED OR AFFIRMED?

For I know the thoughts that I think toward you, says the Lord, thoughts of peace and not of evil, to give you a future and a hope. Then you will call upon Me and go and pray to Me, and I will listen to you. And you will seek Me and find Me, when you search for Me with all your heart. (Jeremiah 29:11–13 NKJV)

1. What are God's thoughts toward you?

2. Fill in the blanks using Jeremiah 29:11 from the verses above. Thoughts of _____ and not of _____, to give you a _____ and a _____.

3. Once we understand the thoughts God has toward us, what does He want us to do according to Jeremiah 29:12 (please fill in the blanks)? Then you will _____ _____ _____ and ___and _____ to _____.'

4. Finally, according to Jeremiah 12:13, God said, "you will seek Him and find Him, when you (fill in the blank) _____ for Me with all your heart."

Lost Discoveries

Would this day be more meaningful to you if you knew there was a purpose and plan in store for you? What if I told you I would grant you a reward of great significance at the end of this month if you completed a set number of tasks within the time frame allotted? Would your priorities be different each day, or would you be passive about how you invest your time, talent, and energy?

What if I also told you there is a divine plan and purpose for every second of every day of your life? What if that plan was in the mind of God as He intentionally created you, knitting you together in your mother's womb and watching you take form and be birthed into this life? He was there, even observing your response to the first sounds you made. I bet His heart skipped a beat when you smiled for the first time. The heavenly hosts probably snickered when your first burp frightened you, and all celebrated the joy of watching you take your first step. Before long, you were running and climbing, and I am quite sure God had to tighten the shift of His angels and earthly guardians He assigned to you.

Over time, you discovered how to dream and became fascinated with His wonderful creation that surrounded you. You explored His creation with all your senses—sight, sound, smell, touch, and taste. The sense of taste eventually became a problem because there was nothing you touched that did not end up in your mouth. You did not understand the concept of wealth or poverty, skin color, or education. None of it mattered to you. Though in reality, your world was very small, your imagination saw vast opportunities that had no limits.

As you grew, your childhood discoveries became bleak and were lost over time. The simple wonder of life that once fascinated you eventually began to mirror the faded dreams of the ones who influenced your life. Was it to their blame? Only God can say. Truth is, the guidance that was provided by the ones who loved you was limited because of their broken pasts. And their pasts were broken because they had not been restored to them by their Creator, God.

How were the pasts of your loved ones broken? That is a great question. This truth is discovered in the garden of Eden. Humankind entered a life of brokenness when Adam made one crucial decision to disobey God. The Bible identifies disobedience as sin. The one decision that was made, which seemed very simple, produced an instinct within our created beings to naturally act against the will, and preference, of our Creator God. So no matter what walk of life you are from—be it of wealth or poverty, of the elect or the outcast—we are all prone to sinful behaviors. We are also in need of a Savior to help us turn from those tendencies, free us from their bondage, and teach us how to live lives free from sin that leads to death.

1. What does James 1:14–15 (NIV say)? Please write it in the spaces below.

2. According to James 1:14, how is each person tempted?

3. What does James 1:15 say happens when desire is conceived?

4. When sin is full grown, what does James 1:15 say it gives birth to?

5. Please write James 4:17 in the space below (use any translation).

6. According to James 4:17, what is it called if anyone knows the good he or she ought to do but does not do it? _____

Defining Moments

Now the LORD God had planted a garden in the east, in Eden; and there he put the man he had formed. The LORD God made all kinds of trees grow out of the ground—trees that were pleasing to the eye and good for food. In the middle of the garden were the tree of life and the tree of the knowledge of good and evil.

The LORD God took the man and put him in the Garden of Eden to work it and take care of it. And the LORD God commanded the man, "You are free to eat from any tree in the garden; but you must not eat from the tree of the knowledge of good and evil, for when you eat from it you will certainly die." (Genesis 2:8-9, 15-17 NIV)

1. Which tree or trees were in the middle of the garden?

2. Did God mention any other trees in the garden? If so, where were they located?

3. Which tree did God command man not to eat from, and where was it located?

The idea is not to point the finger to observe the bad decision that took place here with Adam. Chances increase for any of us to make an unwise choice when we become distracted from truths we have learned or were taught. Poor choices can also be made when we receive a truth that has been slightly altered, which we will see later in this chapter. The overall concept to observe in this portion of scripture is to take a sincere look into our hearts to understand how one moment of compromise can create a lifetime of negative consequences. These are defining moments that set our lives on a course in the direction of God and His best plans for us, or away from Him toward our plans for our lives. Each of us can likely remember a time when we misunderstood a simple instruction, and it resulted in great losses to us over time. Some decisions carry greater consequences if we are not careful to count the costs of their outcomes.

It is easy to cast blame on Adam because of his ignorance regarding the outcome of his decision to disobey God. I can sympathize with Adam and relate to him when I made a choice based on my desire for personal gain and enlightenment and did not consider God's opinion at that moment. When a choice is made to cast blame outward, we fail to realize that we are all broken, we are all imperfect, and we all have deep-rooted sins that need healing (Romans 7:18). Why? Because we were all born into sin because of one decision made by one man (Romans 5:12).

4. Have you ever been given instructions on what to do for any given task, and you altered the instructions to suit an understanding that was later found to be lacking?

5. Once you obtained full knowledge of the original instructions, were you able to see why it was necessary to follow them rather than the altered ones?

6. Are any negative consequences still lingering because of your past misunderstanding?

The Fall of Compromise

When we find ourselves in the normal flow of life's daily activities, it is sometimes easy to compromise or make unwise decisions. Let us consider a scenario.

You have an appointment in a building you are not familiar with. The main entrance is closed, and the detour is not posted at the entrance you were instructed to take. You stop a passing stranger and ask for directions to the office you are looking for. The stranger kindly instructs you to drive to the opposite side of the building and park in the guest parking located to the left of the circle drive. "You will see a set of two glass double doors, walk through them, and turn right. Once inside, you will see an elevator just ahead of you; take it to the fourth floor. When you step off the elevator, turn right, and follow the hall to your left. The office you are looking for should be there."

After thanking the stranger, you hurried to the other side of the building as instructed. You saw a closer parking spot and parked there, not noticing it was reserved. You now had only ten minutes to get the car parked, gather your belongings, and hurry inside the building. You exited your car and headed toward the entrance of the building, where there was only one set of double glass doors. You figured he must have been mistaken. So you decided to ignore the mistake you thought he made and entered the building. Oh no! You were not aware security was performing temperature checks and required face masks to enter the building. You impatiently waited your turn in the line of five people. As you quickly moved forward in the line, you were certain you would still arrive for your meeting in plenty of time. Well, what do you know? The person in front of you decided to protest wearing the mask, which delayed you moving forward in line. The three security guards did not think to pull the guest aside. Instead, they chose to resolve it together. The situation was finally settled. You wore your "Jesus Loves You" T-shirt, and if you misbehaved and showed your frustration, how could you talk about Jesus's love if asked?

OK. You had no temperature, hastily accepted the offered face mask, and then hurried to the elevator. The elevator doors opened, and four people were already inside. According to the sign next to the elevator, there is a four-person maximum. Everyone looked at you with intense stares. You avoided the confrontation and located the stairwell. You walked up the four flights of stairs, opened the door, and entered the hallway. Still following the stranger's directions, you turned right and briskly walked down the hallway. You wondered, *Where are the suite numbers, and why do the doors all have signs posted on them that reads, "Staff Entrance Only"?* There were no windows, and all the doors were locked. And now you were officially late. Whose fault was it?

In your mind, the instructions were followed. And while technically that is true, you chose to compromise. The first mistake you made was entering the wrong side of the building. The stranger said to look for, "two glass double doors." You only saw one set. Next, if you had allowed the extra minute or so for the elevator to return to the first floor, you would have noticed the suite numbers and then easily located the office you were looking for.

And there was another surprise waiting for you when you returned to your car. It was towed because you decided to park in a reserved parking space. Were the compromises worth the efforts that now need to be invested in undoing all the mistakes?

You were allowed to keep your appointment, retrieved your car from the impound, and arrive home for the evening.

Let's consider a more serious thought. Say you've made the decision to commit your life to the Lord, but your heart longs for a companion with whom to serve in this life. Is this an incorrect desire to have? Of course not. The first relationship that God established was the union of Adam and Eve in the garden. Let's say this desire is a strong driving force, and you seem

7

to meet the perfect person, someone with similar passions in ministry and service. Yet there is an unsettling sense in your heart that something is not quite right. But your will seems much stronger than logic.

You decide to submit to your will instead of to the tugging at your heart to consider the things that seem to be wrong. You relax into the relationship. After quite a bit of time has passed, subtle habits have been formed, and your commitments are no longer the same. Passion for the things concerning the church is not as driven, and your reasoning seems very logical at the time. You even exchange forms of intimacy only intended for marriage. But you rationalize them based on the love you believe you have for the person. More time passes, and the relationship ends. You are left with more brokenness, more doubt, and additional wounds that need to be healed.

In both cases, thoughts bombard your mind, accusing you of all the wrong choices you made and how wrong you were for making those choices. But do you see something terribly wrong with this picture? Where were those accusing voices when you were being driven to make those decisions? We never hear the accusing voices until the bad decisions are made. We tend to make decisions based on how we saw others make them when we were growing into adulthood. We learn what we see and do what we learn. And more often than we should, when we decide to make a bad choice, we blame God for the outcome.

> Now the serpent was more crafty than any of the wild animals the Lord God had made. He said to the woman, "Did God really say, 'You must not eat from any tree in the garden'?"
>
> The woman said to the serpent, "We may eat fruit from the trees in the garden, but God did say, 'You must not eat fruit from the tree that is in the middle of the garden, and you must not touch it, or you will die.'"
>
> "You will not certainly die," the serpent said to the woman. "For God knows that when you eat from it your eyes will be opened, and you will be like God, knowing good and evil."
>
> When the woman saw that the fruit of the tree was good for food and pleasing to the eye, and also desirable

for gaining wisdom, she took some and ate it. She also gave some to her husband, who was with her, and he ate it. Then the eyes of both of them were opened, and they realized they were naked; so they sewed fig leaves together and made coverings for themselves.

Then the man and his wife heard the sound of the LORD God as he was walking in the garden in the cool of the day, and they hid from the LORD God among the trees of the garden. But the LORD God called to the man, "Where are you?"

He answered, "I heard you in the garden, and I was afraid because I was naked; so I hid."

And He said, "Who told you that?" (Genesis 3:1–11b NIV)

As time passes, negative choices have a way of robbing us of innocence. The wonder that once lit a flame in one's imagination suddenly dims and slowly fades away. We start to believe that all the dreams we had during childhood were not a reality, and we become convinced of our poverty of hope. The Word of God says we are fearfully and wonderfully made (Psalm 139:14), but we have learned how to dislike the uniqueness of our personalities, the sounds of our voices, the shapes of our bodies, or maybe something else about ourselves that we're convinced is a deformity.

In Genesis 3:8 (NIV), the Bible says, Adam and his wife Eve, "heard the sound of the Lord God as he was walking in the garden in the cool of the day." Going with the context of scripture in the previous verses, one could conclude Adam and Eve would eagerly greet the Lord on hearing His presence. What caused this day to be different? The Bible goes on to say, "The Lord called to the man and asked, 'Where are you?'" (Genesis 3:9). Imagine you have a beautiful relationship with a spouse, friend, parent, or child. Then one day you come to visit, and that person hides from you because he or she is now afraid of you.

In Genesis 3:10, fear was introduced into our lives because of sin. What was the offense Adam caused against God? He ate of the fruit of the tree that God told him not to eat of (Genesis 2:16, 17). Why was this such a bad thing to do? It was only fruit, right? Was it?

As an adult, you have naturally accrued more wisdom in knowledge and experience than children have. When you add education to the equation, you possess a level of wisdom children will not be able to comprehend with the intellect they currently have. Thinking as a mature adult, if you instruct children not to do something, it is usually to protect them from a danger they do not understand. Here in this story with God, Adam, and Eve, shame and fear were introduced by an outsider that deliberately meant them harm. I encourage you to read Genesis 2:5–25 and 3:1–13 for additional context.

1. Can you think of a decision you made and acted on, and your life has never been the same since? What was it, and how has your life changed?

> There is a way that seems right to a man, but its end is the way of death. (Proverbs 14:12 NKJV)

Well, one would rightly question, what is the right way to live?

God's Unchanged Plan

God still has a plan for your life. But it is clear that Satan has one for you also. For me, the enemy of my soul had an advantage of influence in my early teenage years. The seeds planted in my life as a child started to manifest through my behaviors. I have volunteered and worked with children in some capacity for roughly fifteen years. When it comes to behaviors, I have noticed their discipline, speech, and gestures resemble the key influencers in their lives, be it a parent, a classroom buddy, or even a teacher. As a child, I started to imitate the behaviors I saw around me, the behaviors of well-meaning family members and friends who surrounded me. Unfortunately, I was not a reflection of the Lord.

Very early in my teenage years, my actions started to imitate the ways of the influencers in my life. What I did not understand at the time was that my actions would produce a negative outcome, which would result in another unfruitful action to repair the previous outcome. It started me on a dark, slippery slope further away from the Father's plan for me.

As I expressed in my previous book, *A Shadow of Death*, I was taught to always go to church. I knew enough about God, to respect Him, and I heard He loved me. But considering the environment I grew up in, my concept of love was very flawed. So how can one grasp the understanding of the type of love that comes from a God who is respected but has limited understanding of who He is? So yes, the enemy was busy planning and prodding for my life. But God was also busy at work, planting His seeds that eventually produced a life content in Him.

I eventually gave God my passions, which He later revived into His predesigned plan instilled within me. That atmosphere was used to draw me deeper into a relationship with Him so He could shape my life to eventually become who He designed me to be.

> I was the youngest of three children. My mother was single and worked two and sometimes three jobs to make ends meet for us financially. My biological father was not present in my life …
>
> I have memories of living with my mother, grandmother, aunt, and cousins. (from *A Shadow of Death*)

Because I had frequent changes in residences, I lacked a personal space that belonged only to me. My bedroom, closet, and dresser drawer were always shared or borrowed. My belongings were often in a bag piled in a corner, or a shared space with someone. Somehow, in all my transitioning from house to house, I eventually ended up back with my mother in my late teenage years. Around that time, an incident happened while I was out with friends. We were all drinking and partying during the summer, when activities were very limited in the town where I was born and was living at the time. After a while, I had a bit too much to drink and decided to provoke a fight with an acquaintance over something I disagreed with. Because of my arrogance, I persisted in bullying her until she was forced to respond to my intimidation. The outcome was not very favorable for me. She hit me in my lip, which became very swollen and needed to be cared for. They took me to the home of a trusted loved one, who opened the door, saw my state, and closed it, offering us no assistance. My heart was crushed, but my pride would not allow me to feel the emotion of rejection that was growing into a massive crop within me.

During that time, I was working at a local fast-food restaurant and would receive my first and only paycheck within a few days. I contacted my ex-sister-in-law, who was living in a different state, and she welcomed me to live with her and her family. I crashed at the home of a friend for a couple days and then purchased a bus ticket. And off I went. All my possessions were in two trash bags, and I had no idea how my life was getting ready to make significant changes.

Instead of feeling that I was confirmed and accepted by others, I learned how to feel the opposite—disapproval and rejection. I do not believe these individuals intentionally purposed in their hearts to impress these emotions upon me, nor did they have any idea they were doing so. But it happened and set me on a course that would require the grace of God to establish many new beginnings.

1. What is your initial impression of a bad experience?

2. How often do you find yourself repeating a bad experience before you are forced to change?

3. Once you decide to change (the way you think, your friendships, place of residence, and so on), do you have regrets about not doing so sooner?

Look Again

One could take a long, hard look at the circumstances above and feel a form of sadness for the individual. That is natural. Unfortunately, we live in a world where our lives have strayed significantly away from the family structure of God.

The Bible teaches us in Psalm 127:3 (NIV) that children are a heritage from the Lord. It also teaches us that fathers (*parents*) do not (*should not*) provoke your children to anger but bring them up in the discipline and instruction of the Lord (Ephesians 6:4 NIV). If you train up a child in the way he or she should go; even when the child is old, he or she will not depart from it (Proverbs 22:6 ESV). The Word of God is truth, even if children suddenly decide to rebel against the proper standards you previously instilled within them. If you remain true to discovering your children's God-given gifts and talents and trust Him to show you how to train them, the Word will eventually produce a harvest in their lives according to the plan that God intended it to be.

But what happens in the family when there is a breakdown in the structure and order the Lord originally intended for it? For so long the enemy placed a label of shame upon my life for not being raised in a traditional family. I did not have the godly teachings and disciplines, according to scripture, from my father and mother. Nor did I have consistent relationships with them. Because of this, my emotional struggles have been very difficult. But we do serve a good God. He said He would be a, "Father to the fatherless and a defender of widows" (Psalm 68:5 NIV). Today, I can confess that He has been just that to me, a faithful Father.

Would my life be different today if I were raised up how the Lord intended? Would I have brought more respect and honor to my mother and stepfather than I did when I was a child? Probably. But today, the only certain thing I am aware of is how my choices today can affect the future of my family and friends tomorrow. My part is to "love the Lord (my) God with all (my) heart and with all (my) soul and with all (my) mind (Matthew 22:37 NIV). And if possible, so far as it depends on me, live peaceably with all (Romans 12:18 NIV) and trust God to do the rest.

If I could hear God speaking to the person I was then, this is how I believe He was encouraging her:

Dear Beloved,

What if I told you that there is a plan for your life? I completely understand your heartbreaks, and it is very difficult for you to see My plan for your life right now. What I can tell you is one day, you will feel the acceptance that you now so desperately long for. One day you will find yourself quite content and discover true love in Me like you cannot begin to imagine. Not only will your natural family be one day united, you will also have a family of brothers and sisters more numerous than your mind can imagine.

> So, then you are no longer strangers and aliens, but you are fellow citizens with the saints and members of the household of God, built on the foundation of the apostles and prophets, Christ Jesus himself being the cornerstone, in whom the whole structure, being joined together, grows into a holy temple in the Lord. In him you also are being built together into a dwelling place for God by the Spirit. (Ephesians 2:19–22 NASB)

My sweet child, this is your inheritance in Me.

Yes, you will experience a few heartbreaks along the way, and you will make many more bad choices. But because I, your heavenly Father, love you, I will use those choices to help shape your character. Some day you will also have a home of your own. One that you will secure with the resources I will provide. Through you, I will cause many others to have furnished homes, clothes on their backs, and satisfied bellies. You will one day be My hands to care for and give to the hopeless, you will be My feet and mouth to carry and proclaim the gospel. Everything you lack, I will cause you to be to others. In the things that you now feel hopeless, I will heal you while you are taking My hope to the broken.

Do not lose hope. You are not, nor will you ever be alone; you are deeply loved. Can't you see it? One day soon, I will provide streams in the desert places of your life, make a roadway in the wilderness, and provide rivers that you have not known—as long as you abide in Me, your Creator.

Surrender to My plan for your life. Allow yourself to trust in Me, and most important, learn how to dream again.

Love,
Your heavenly Father, the One who redeemed you.

QUESTIONS TO PONDER

1. Has anything happened to you that made or makes you feel rejected? Being specific, write it down and the person or situation that caused it.

2. What did you do in response to that feeling of rejection?

3. Today, do you think your response should have been different? Why or why not?

4. Are you practicing the same sin that was committed toward you to others, or are you practicing the affirmation that you wanted to receive? Please explain.

   Note: If someone came to mind after you read this question, that is the person you may need to show a little more grace to.

5. How many people have you rejected because of the sin of rejection done toward you? Write their names in the space below.

Extra Mile: Write down a special prayer for the people who inflicted the sin of rejection upon you and the names of those you have rejected. Do not be afraid to be transparent before the Father. He longs to be intimately involved in all that concerns you. Take as much time as you need to be sincere with Him. (Use the "Additional Notes" section found on the page that follows.)

ADDITIONAL NOTES

_____

_____

_____

_____

_____

_____

_____

_____

_____

_____

_____

_____

_____

_____

_____

_____

_____

HUMILIATED OR APPRECIATED?

The Lord bless you and keep you; the Lord make his face shine on you and be gracious to you; the Lord turn his face toward you and give you peace. (Numbers 6:24-26 NIV)

Now that I was relocating to a different state, was I running away from a problem that needed to be dealt with, or was I running toward an opportunity that would better situate a positive future for me? In that moment, when I made the decision to move, I cannot tell you if I was even considering that question. Today, I believe it was the best decision that I made for myself during that time. I was on a harsh path of destruction and receiving no firm guidance toward a better direction. One would say it was how I wanted to live my life, so I was allowed to do and live as I pleased. Today I would challenge that thought. As a teenager, was it about what I *wanted,* or should it have been more of what I *needed*?

During that time in my life, I needed to feel loved and affirmed instead of rejected. Ironically, I found a hint of that affirmation among the crowd of friends who were teaching me the way of destruction through drinking and heavy partying. Today I can also see that God did grant me a ray of light. I believe He used the opportunity of relocation to set me on a different path and to teach me a better way. He was there with me even in my pain and even when I was His enemy. At that time, I did not accept Him as Lord. Instead, I was making myself lord of my life and causing more harm than good. Yet Jesus remained steadfast and respectfully stood at the door of my life, gently nudging my heart for me to let Him in.

> Behold, I stand at the door and knock. If anyone hears my voice and opens the door, I will come in to him and eat with him, and he with me. (Revelation 3:20 ESV)

1. Can you think of a defining moment in your past that set your life on a different path (good or bad)? Please explain.

2. Have you forgiven the person or people who forced you on that path?

3. Are you willing to trust God to heal you of the grief they caused you?

4. Do you believe God was there with you, even in that moment of pain inflicted upon you?

There Is a Way That Seems Right

Today I can see how much my ex-sister-in-law (we will call her Tracy) was a blessing to me, even though neither one of us saw it at the time. I believe God used her as a doorway of opportunity into a better life for me. No, she was not a Christian at the time, but she has always had a kind and generous heart since I have known her. Tracy was my brother's former girlfriend and bore him two beautiful children. She had moved away from our hometown and on with her life, which included a relationship with someone else. There was no reason for her to help or support me, yet she did. And I am grateful. I felt welcomed into her life, and she expected nothing in return from me. I looked up to her and valued our friendship. I still do.

Tracy helped guide my life at a time when I was very fragile and needed assurance that there was still hope in life. She arranged time in her schedule to help me find a job and an apartment. I even met a hot guy. The guy thing was all my doing, and boy, did I end up with many regrets for this decision. You will understand why shortly.

> But while everyone was sleeping, his enemy came and sowed weeds among the wheat, and went away. (Matthew 13:25 NIV)

Interesting thought: Sin never shows up in its fully manifested form. It is always presented as a suggestion, a thought, or a recommendation from a trusted individual. Before the act of sin is committed, have you noticed you never feel guilt or shame or hear the nagging voice of accusation in your head about the act you are getting ready to commit? These emotions only show up *after* the act of sin is committed.

1. Can you think of a time when a so-called great opportunity was presented to you, but you later realized it was a trap leading to the act of sin and ultimately harsh consequences?

2. How did God provide a way out?

Entanglements of a Desire

Let us call him Sam. Who is Sam? The "hot guy," remember? We met through a mutual friend. He was very quiet, reserved, and smiled a lot. He started to ask our friend questions about me, and she would later tell me all he was asking. Sometime later, he worked up the nerve to ask me out, and I gladly accepted. By this time, I had become very fond of him and was quite curious to know him better. We started to spend a lot of time together, hanging out at my apartment or attending various outings with friends or his family members. He seemed to know exactly what I wanted in a relationship and had a unique way of making me feel that I was the center of his world.

After dating for a while, I thought it to be a good idea to allow him to move in with me since we were spending so much time together. I feel the need to remind you, I was not a Christian during this time; God was only a part of my Sunday morning schedule. We purchased a dog together, and I believed this young man was all I ever wanted. What I did not realize at the time was how we slowly stopped hanging with our friends and only attended his family functions or go on outings that only involved the two of us. Church was no longer a priority to me because he wanted me to spend this time with him and his family. He eventually convinced me to quit my job because he wanted to take care of me. And I did. But as time passed, I became jaded about waiting for him to return home or bored while waiting for him at his mother's home. I soon decided to return to work, not imagining the friction it would cause between the two of us.

Looking back, I now see how God provided me a life vest through my friendship with Tracy, which saved me from drowning in the circumstances that I left in my hometown. Because I had not learned to deal with the internal pain and offenses, distractions were bound to recur. I was easily lured away from the progress that was taking place in my life through her and into a fantasy world I thought I was equipped to manage. I had not yet discovered a way to heal my feelings of rejection in the Lord. So what did I choose to do instead? I continued to look for affirmation from people.

1. Do you still carry unresolved pain or offense in your heart from someone in your past? If so, what is it, and who is it toward?

2. What are you using to sooth the ache that is still present from the pain or offense?

The Raging War

I got a part-time job and found myself quite content. This decision only worsened my relationship with Sam and brought no help to it at all. Our relationship spiraled drastically. It quickly became clear to me that I was not in a good place with him, and I desperately began to look for ways out.

Growing up, I witnessed firsthand unhealthy relationships that were verbally and physically degrading. The harm these relationships do to someone is lasting in its effects. Some people never recover from the devastation. As an outsider looking into those types of relationships, one would confidently believe separation from the individual is a simple choice. However, the individual experiencing the hardships of it daily could argue that the decision to leave is not that simple. Once the mind is trapped inside a belief and everything about the environment supports that belief, the circumstances become that person's reality. This was the case I found myself at that time of my life.

Some of the things I experienced I would have never imagined being a part of my life. I even learned emotional defenses to prevent those circumstances from taking place. The type of life I had been avoiding was now my reality, and I honestly saw no way forward. All attempts I tried to better myself were found not to be good enough, or it was assumed that there was an ulterior motive behind my gesture. I felt trapped under a thumb of criticism. Anger and bitterness welled massively within me, and they needed an outlet.

After a series of not-so-wonderful events had taken place, I discovered a way out of the relationship with Sam. I took with me more scars and deeper wounds than I previously experienced. I became angry with myself and really did not like the person I had become. I eventually spiraled deeply into drinking. All my spare time was spent in a bar, an after-party at my house or someone else's, or an outdoor activity where alcohol was a definite part of the agenda. I would find employment that had weekly payouts or server positions to fund my habit. I met new friends at the bars I frequented because my relationship had slowly isolated me from the friends I previously had. I even allowed him to isolate me from Tracy over time. The failed relationship with Sam eventually left me with an "I told you so" mentality. I started to wonder if there was a point in trying to have consistency and loyalty in my life as I had convinced myself that no one was ever consistent and loyal to me. I was in a cycle of passionately giving away to someone else what I so desperately desired.

I was not in a good place emotionally. But despite the raging war taking place within me, something was there, pulling in a different direction, trying to lead me away from self-harm and into a place of rest. A rest from trying to obtain something without God, something that I had not yet learned with Him. Today I know that God was nudging me in His direction. But my soul could not hear Him because of the noise that surrounded me. So I reached for what seemed right to me during that time of need. I again became faithful in my church attendance, and though I could not see it at the time, my life was beginning to take shape. Hints of beauty were beginning to form within the ashes. True, this separation was the cause of my spiral, but was I spiraling out of control or closer to becoming in control?

My desires had become my adversaries, leading me further into a deep pit of darkness. I am grateful for the resilience that I had begun to develop, even though I did not realize it at the time. Though my life was spiraling further away from God, I know that He was still there with me during my bad choices. While I was still a sinner, Jesus died for me (Romans 5:8). Now, though the seeds of rejection and humiliation had taken root, God still had a plan for my life. His love never stopped calling out to me even though my will dominated my resistance to Him.

> Enter through the narrow gate. For wide is the gate and broad is the road that leads to destruction, and many enter through it. But small is the gate and narrow the road that leads to life, and only a few find it. (Matthew 7:13–14 NIV)

Two Roads before Me

Two unfamiliar roads before me, I know not which way to go.
My eyes peered towards their end; my heart was desperate to know.
One seemed wide and well-groomed, its lure seemed familiar and true.
The other was narrow and overgrown, creating a resistance to its pursuit.

I succumbed to the familiar, never to imagine
the traps and deep pits it held.
I fell prey to some of its darkness; all the details I will never tell.

Afraid and badly bruised, I was guided toward a comforting light.
It drew me toward another path, narrower than the
one on which I had previously taken flight.

As I journeyed, new outlooks consumed me,
and I was filled with much intrigue.
Oh, the journey ahead, my mind knows not what it will be.

Lead me, Jesus, by the light of Your Word. Wash
me with Your love, and make me new.

1. Please write out Ephesians 5:26 in the space below.

QUESTIONS TO PONDER

1. Can you think of anything in your past that hurt or disappointed you, and you then became that very thing to someone else? Examples: Someone failed to be loyal to you, and now you fail to be loyal to others. Or you or someone you know were abused, and now you abuse or have chosen to accept abuse.

2. What understanding do you have today that changes your opinion about the moments experienced or witnessed in the answer you wrote for question 1?

3. In your opinion, why do hurting people hurt other people when they understand the pain that is being inflicted?

4. Consider skipping this question if you are not willing to answer it truthfully. The question is: Do you want to change?

If you answered yes to question 4, pray this prayer or write your own in the space provided in the "Additional Notes" section on the following pages.

But before we pray, understand that change is impossible within your ability. How many times have you tried to change yourself and failed? We were not designed to walk through this life alone, weighed down by all its worries. There is a way to receive peace and freedom from the bondage of sin. The way is with God the Father, through His Son, Jesus Christ. John 3:16 (ESV) says, "For God so loved the world, that He gave His only Son, so that everyone who believes in Him will not perish, but have eternal life." Eternal life is salvation, which is an eternity with God. The sanctification process takes place in Jesus Christ when you allow Him to become Lord of your life. How do you make Jesus Lord of your life? The Bible teaches us in Romans 10:9 (NKJV), "that if you confess with your mouth Jesus as Lord, and believe in your heart that God raised Him from the dead, you will be saved." Jesus also promised in John 14:26 (NKJV) that "the Helper, the Holy Spirit, whom the Father will send in My name, He will teach you all things, and bring to your remembrance all things that I said to you."

You never have to be alone again.

If you have already given Jesus Lordship over your life, then pray this prayer or go the extra mile and write your own in the "Additional Notes" section on the following page.

> Heavenly Father, thank You for showing me my need for change. Thank You for revealing to me the hurt inflicted upon me by other hurting people. Today I choose to forgive them for the sin they committed toward me. Lord, I ask that You forgive me for the times I caused hurt and pain back to them and others. Grant me the strength to make amends with them in hopes of reconciliation or a peaceful relationship with them. Create in me a pure heart, O God, and renew a steadfast spirit within me. You promised that Your grace would be sufficient for me, and Your power is made perfect in weakness. Father, I am weak before You, and I pray for the strength of Your grace and power. Grant me a new heart, and put a new spirit in me. Remove from me my heart of stone, and give me a heart of flesh. May my life bring You glory. In Jesus's name I pray. Amen.

If you would like to accept Jesus as Lord, please audibly repeat the following prayer.

> God, thank You for the gift of salvation that You provided through Jesus. I confess that I am a sinner who needs a

Savior. I confess Jesus is Lord, and I believe in my heart that You, God, raised Him from the dead. Forgive me of my sins, and heal me of my brokenness. In Jesus's name, Amen.

Please write out 2 Corinthians 12:9 in the space below.

5. Do you believe this verse is true for you? Why or why not?

Please write out Psalm 51:10 in the space below.

6. Is this your desire from the Lord? If not, what do you think is hindering you from this desire?

Please write out Ezekiel 36:26 in the space below.

7. Think of a recurring ache in your heart. Now allow some time to imagine having a new and freeing outlook on this situation. Do you believe God can heal you?

ADDITIONAL NOTES

_____

_____

_____

_____

_____

_____

_____

_____

_____

_____

_____

_____

_____

_____

_____

_____

_____

INTRIGUE OR ENSNARING DECEPTIONS?

Simon, Simon, Satan has asked to sift all of you as wheat. (Luke 22:31 NIV)

> As a young adult, everything about my life reflected rebellion, hostility, anger, and disobedience; ... Often, I would pass the time engaging in senseless, mind-numbing activities; to distract my thoughts from my reality, so I turned to the next drink. (from *A Shadow of Death*)

During this point in my life, I was more lost than ever. There was a longing within me that I could not relate to, and I had no one in my life to show me what my true need was. I no longer understood my emotions, and I had a deep thirst and hunger to be filled. But I had no idea what that satisfaction looked like.

> Blessed are those who hunger and thirst for righteousness,
> for they will be filled. (Matthew 5:6 NIV)

The war became so consuming, as did the desire for more understanding of my need. Finally, I believed the only thing to silence it was to drown out the noise with drinking. Life was no longer enjoyable; there was no pleasantness to speak of, and my view of personal value had tanked to an all-time low. Now insecure because of my feelings of rejection and shame through humiliation, I discovered new and comforting pleasure through high consumption of alcohol. I looked forward to drinking every day, and I started to gravitate toward people who shared those same values. But on Sunday mornings, though I knew I still reeked of alcohol and probably looked like I came out of a horror movie, something continued to lure me to church. I would find the most obscure places within the congregation where I could sit and enjoy a moment of stillness. Then I quickly escaped the fellowship afterward the service. Attending church was the only time the accusing voices in my mind seemed to be silenced. I was not aware if I was noticed by anyone. Nor did I really care at the time because of the low opinion I had of myself. For reasons I could not explain, during the moments I spent sitting and listening to the services, it seemed as though I was in a state of waiting. It was the only place I felt at rest and able to let my defenses down. I felt a sense of comfort and safety that I was not familiar with, which seemed to escape me when I went back to my familiar environment. I was still ignorant of the fact that I was in desperate need of a Savior to free me from the entanglement of my sins. Instead, I continued to depend on another drink to relieve me from the emotional anguish.

> Do not get drunk on wine, which leads to debauchery.
> Instead, be filled with the Spirit. (Ephesians 5:18 NIV)

When I engaged in drinking, I did not try to control the amount I consumed; my goal was to get as drunk as possible. I never worried about the consequences or dangers I was putting myself or others in. I never swore that I would cut back or stop. It was a conscious and intentional activity I practiced.

There are various forms of addictions. All of them lead to mental imprisonment and could cause physical demise if not properly dealt with. Other than alcohol, there were other addictions I could have easily been ensnared by, but a part of my heart knew to reject them. Curious to understand why I chose to drink as my escape, I decided to research the topic of alcoholism from a secular viewpoint.

I stumbled upon an online article written by Elliot Redwine explaining the progressive conditions of the different stages of alcoholism. According to Redwine, the stages include:

1. Pre-alcoholic stage
2. Early-stage alcoholism
3. Middle alcoholic phase
4. End-stage alcoholism

He goes on to explain that "no two individuals have identical reasons that lead them to develop alcohol use disorder. Despite the variation in specific causes and timeframes from person to person, the disease itself follows a pattern."

To explain the pattern in depth, he references the Jellinek curve theory. This study illustrates the symptoms seen during a person's progression through four stages of alcoholism.

After closely evaluating the four stages, I concluded I was in the early stages of alcoholism, which was stage 2. The signs he listed included:

- Regular binge drinking
- Blacking out (memory loss caused by drinking)

- Difficulties controlling the amount they drink
- Swearing they will cut back or stop but having trouble doing so

Philippians 3:17 (ESV) reads, "join in imitating me, and keep your eyes on those who walk according to the example you have in us." In relation to this verse, the answer to my previous question as to why I chose this form of addiction was simple: I became what I observed. The examples I had as a child and through my teenage years were environments in which alcohol and parties that were extremely accessible. The seed was planted long before I realized the power of its influence over my life. We simply do what we learn, and we learn what we are taught, whether the habits are good or bad. Thanks be to God for His mercy. I praise Him for pursuing me, even when I was in my darkest pit of despair.

> Where can I go from Your Spirit? Or where can I flee from Your presence? If I ascend to heaven, You are there; If I make my bed in Sheol, behold, You are there. If I take up the wings of the dawn, If I dwell in the remotest part of the sea, even there Your hand will lead me, and Your right hand will take hold of me. If I say, "Surely the darkness will overwhelm me, and the light around me will be night," even darkness is not dark to You, and the night is as bright as the day. Darkness and light are alike to You. (Psalm 139:7–12 NASB)

1. Research the *Merriam Webster* online definition of the word *addiction* and write it in the space below.

2. What addictions have you struggled with or are struggling with today?

3. Think of the main influencers as a child. Write their names in the space provided below.

4. Did/do they struggle with the same addictions you listed for question 2?

The Lure of Temptation

Blessed *is* the man who endures temptation; for when he has been approved, he will receive the crown of life which the Lord has promised to those who love Him. Let no one say when he is tempted, "I am tempted by God"; for God cannot be tempted by evil, nor does He Himself tempt anyone. But each one is tempted when he is drawn away by his own desires and enticed. (James 1:12–14 NKJV)

Today I can see how my soul was crying out for help because I was so close to utter defeat. One tangled web eventually branched off to a neighboring one hidden in an area of my heart to which I was completely blinded.

Time passed, and Sam started to phase out of my life. I discovered a new skill within me and perfected it, which was learning how to hide from him. Praise God social media was not popular during this time, so staying under the radar to avoid him became easy to do. Eventually, I found another place of employment and started to develop new friendships with my coworkers. One of them invited me to a club after work, where homosexual relationships were very open. I had gotten to know her, and there was always a level of respect for our beliefs within our employment relationship. I was a bit hesitant at first. Even for me, this was a little extreme. But my coworker was persistent in her invite, enticing me with the club's weekly beer specials. One evening she invited me to go with her to the club's "silver coin night." One night a week you could get beer for any silver coin. This beer special absolutely blew my mind! I was more intrigued by it and was convinced there must be a gimmick involved to recover their profits. I went, anticipating the catch, like watered-down tap beer. But the special was what it said. A person could give any silver coin to buy any bottled beer. Today, that is unheard of. Well, you better believe this was my new hangout spot and my new favorite night of the week.

During that first night, a girl caught my attention. I will call her Kim. She was sitting alone at a table next to the dance floor. She was grooving along to the beat of the music, seeming to be content alone with herself. During my observation of her, I noticed she was not at the bar alone. She was with a group of friends who were dancing, but Kim did not seem to have interest in dancing with them. Her contentment intrigued me, and I became so impressed by it that I became envious. Why? I did not know how to be in a state of contentment alone with myself. Relationships, activities, and other people identified who I was as a person, and at that time, I did not know anything different.

The group of friends I was partying with promptly regained my attention, and my previous thoughts soon left my mind. Later that night I went for another beer, and I bumped into someone who would soon become a significant part of my life. We started to engage in an intriguing dialogue. As our conversation progressed, I learned she was getting out of a similar type of relationship that I had with Sam. Over time, several months later, our relationship progressed significantly. We went as far as moving in together, and I shared my newfound love with my family. Though the void of true satisfaction never went away, I somehow felt content in my understanding of what completeness was to me at that time.

We had many friends, and our social activities were at an all-time high. It was like I had discovered a world where there was complete freedom and a lack of judgment. No one cared what type of job I held or the size of my home. My family history was not important; nor did my educational background have relevance. I was embraced within a community that saw past my imperfections and treated me as though I was family. Yet, why was my thirst not satisfied? Why did the longing for more out of life intensify within me? I continued to go to church and started to take Kim with me.

We eventually moved further out of the city because we both felt the need to hide from our ex-lovers. Our isolation from them also moved us quite a way from the bars, making the travel home unsafe after drinking huge amounts of alcohol, especially at the rate we consumed it. Surprisingly I had become a homebody. I found a decent job in the community we were living in and was trying to be a domesticated woman. Go figure. Kim's parents later decided she needed to move from the state we were living in to one much closer to them as they were both older. She invited me to go with her, and so I went.

1. Have you ever found yourself freed from one type of bondage yet later find yourself ensnared in a similar one? Please explain.

2. Have you ever been intrigued by something that you now see was a form of deception? If so, what was it?

3. If you answered question 2, can you now see what your real need was during that time?

Beauty for My Ashes

And provide for those who grieve in Zion—to bestow on them
a crown of beauty instead of ashes, the oil of joy instead of
mourning, and a garment of praise instead of a spirit of despair.
They will be called oaks of righteousness, a planting of the
Lord for the display of his splendor. (Isaiah 61:3 NIV)

Months before our move, God decided it was time to get me saved and baptized. Yep, you heard me right, saved and baptized. Almost immediately, I started to notice a new type of consciousness within my heart regarding the lifestyle I was living with Kim. Today I can see that it was the Holy Spirit, nudging me away from the path of destruction I was on. Not just in my relationship with her, but with my overall decisions in life. I no longer felt comfortable with the choices I was making, beginning with our relationship. Through scripture, it eventually became clear to me that the lifestyle I was living was not righteous in God's eyes. Today, my position statement regarding sexuality is found in one of two life-enhancing options according to the following scriptures. I can either live a monogamous marital relationship, which is between one man and one woman (Genesis 1:27–28; 2:18, 21–24; Matthew 19:4–6; Mark 10:5–8) or choose sexual celibacy (1 Corinthians 7:7; Matthew 19:12). Either of the two is a precious gift from God that is given as He wills to the individual.

I can now see how I eventually released one aspect of desire in my relationship with Sam and clung to another one with Kim. I did not know how to properly heal. Nor was I aware that I was masking deeply rooted trauma from my past. I reached for pleasures that made sense to me at the time, but I was blind to the cycles of destruction that came with them. On the surface, how I presented myself to others and the things and people I surrounded myself with, I appeared to be happy and finally making progress in life. Yet inside, I was still full of insecurity and shame. My relationship with Jesus introduced me to beauty for my ashes of the past, the ashes of abandonment, rejection, abuse, and neglect. I finally found what I was desperately looking for in a relationship with Jesus Christ. I had accepted my salvation in Him and was redeemed by His blood, and it was now time for Him to continue the sanctification process and shape me more in His image. I praise Him that I no longer have to live a life of despair over my past because He has promised to give me joy.

Using the NASB version of the Bible, please fill in the blanks:

1. Hebrews 13:12: "Therefore Jesus also _____ outside the gate, that He might _____ the _____ through _____ _____ _____."

2. 2 Corinthians 7:1: "Therefore, since we have these promises, dear friends, let us _____ _____ from _____ that _____ body and spirit, _____ _____ out of _____ for _____."

3. 2 Timothy 2:21: "Those who _____ themselves from the latter will be _____ for _____ _____, made _____, useful to the Master and _____ to _____ any _____ _____."

All Things New

One fine Sunday morning, while hung-over from the night before, I was sitting in City Church of Oklahoma City, Oklahoma. Then suddenly, I heard the Pastor say, "Would you like to give your life to the Lord Jesus today?" That's all I remember as I said to myself, *Why not?* That day I stood up, accepted Jesus into my heart, confessed that He is Lord and repented of my sinful behaviors, and knew that I was in desperate need of a Savior.

Time passed, and I joined a small group and found true love among strangers. For the first time, I was not as concerned about someone taking care of my momentary needs, which satisfied unhealthy behaviors; instead, someone spoke to my spiritual needs. This experience was a first, and I liked it. I decided to get baptized. (from *A Shadow of Death*)

1. Write out the verse for 1 Corinthians 12:27 in the space below.

2. Fill in the blanks using Colossians 1:18 (NIV): "And he (Jesus) is the _____ of the body, _____; he (Jesus) is the _____ and the _____ from among the dead, so that in everything he (Jesus) might have the _____."

3. Do you agree with question 2? _____ Why or why not?

4. Write out the verse for Ephesians 2:19–22 in the space below.

> I appeal to you therefore, brothers, by the mercies of God, to present your bodies as a living sacrifice, holy and acceptable to God, which is your spiritual worship. Do not be conformed to this world, but be transformed by the renewal of your mind, that by testing you may discern what is the will of God, what is good and acceptable and perfect. (Romans 12:1–2 ESV)

God eventually healed me, starting with my mind. He used the small group that I was attending to disciple me in His Word. I began to learn who He really was intimately. I later learned of His love for me, though I struggled greatly in accepting this truth. His Word taught me that I was free to live a life of purity, and my true desires could only first be discovered in Him. Over time, I have discovered the intimacy of conversation, fullness, and security in knowing He will never abandon me. An intimacy of His loving rebukes and correction because He wants me to fulfill my highest good. My soul blesses Him for His mercy, compassion, and grace. The Lord truly is good, and His love endures forever.

> Start children off on the way they should go, and even when they are old they will not turn from it. (Proverbs 22:6 NIV)

As for the decision to accept Jesus as my Lord, I do not believe it was a decision made in that single moment. I believe God was ministering to my heart during all the Sundays I sat in the stillness of the services. I believe faith was developing within me by hearing the Word of God (Romans 10:17) being ministered by the preacher. I also believe, to this day, that someone was praying for me.

According to Proverbs 22:6, is this a guarantee for everyone? What about the children who were faithfully taught the Word of God but later in life confess atheism? What about the individuals who unfortunately lose their lives to violent crimes or their various types of addictions and never find their ways into a relationship with Jesus as Lord of their lives? My heart breaks with all these realities, but in the end, each of us has free will. When we are of age, we develop an ability to reason rationally. We also possess the freedom to exercise free will, which allows everyone to choose a path that will either take us in the direction of God or away from Him. He desires that we choose life in Jesus (John 10:10). We each must come to the reality that we are powerless in this life without a savior. Still today, after many consistent years in a relationship with the Lord, I find myself powerless without His guidance in my life.

Does Proverbs 22:6 imply that we shape children into an image of the dreams we had for ourselves? Of course not. As Christians, if we confess belief in Jeremiah 29:11, then we will prayerfully seek God to learn how He desires for us to raise the children He has entrusted unto us. We learn to look for gifts early in their lives and attempt to discover whether they are leaders or followers. We attempt to recognize if they have teacher qualities within them, identify the gift of serving others, or maybe they have a love for administration.

> For just as we have many parts in one body and all the body's parts do not have the same function, so we, who are many, are one body in Christ, and individually parts of one another. However, since we have gifts that differ according to the grace given to us, each of us is to use them properly: if prophecy, in proportion to one's faith; if service, in the act of serving; or the one who teaches, in the act of teaching; or the one who exhorts, in the work of exhortation; the one who gives, with generosity; the one who is in leadership, with diligence; the one who shows mercy, with cheerfulness. (Romans 12:4–8 NASB)

What does this information about training up children have to do with my relationship with God the Father, in Jesus, and the difficulties of my past? Everything. A discovery of purpose does not guarantee a life of perfection. I believe if my God-given gifts were recognized as a child and developed throughout my teenage years, I most likely would have been placed on a path that leads to His righteousness. I am sure there would have been twists and turns along the way, but the pathways through darkness may not have left behind so many regrets and painful memories. Would my life be different today? Only God knows. Were my parents or other adults in my life wrong for the decisions they made for me when I was a child? Only God can be the judge of that. My part is to accept life as it is today and make better choices for my tomorrows, which are found in loving the Lord with all my heart.

> Trust in the Lord with all your heart and do not lean on your own understanding. (Proverbs 3:5 NASB)

Well, what does loving God with all my heart and not leaning on my understanding look like? Let us consider a job opportunity that matched my skill sets and passions in life. My commute to and from work would be quite convenient, and the working hours and pay rate were very suitable for my expectations. I did my due diligence and prepared for the interview but was not selected for the position. All my intentions were great. I prayed, had the skills the employer was looking for, experience, education, and hopefully the proper presentation of myself to reflect the culture of the company. But I was not chosen. Was this God's fault? If not, then whose fault was it? Well, I would say it was no one's fault. Someone else was just a better fit for the position, and if that place of employment were a part of God's plan for my life, He would have opened a door of opportunity for me to serve Him in that place of employment.

So what did I do? I continued to pray, continued to love Him, and continued to seek His wisdom concerning the paths He has ordained for my life. Though painful at times, I am learning how to trust God's decision for closing certain doors of opportunity and opening others I was not aware of.

QUESTIONS TO PONDER

1. Looking back over your life, can you recall a moment when a deception lured you away from what you knew was best, and in the end, it led you to more chaos?

2. How did you break free from the entanglement of its grip?

3. Can you see that God's presence was there with you even though you never really considered His help for freedom from it? _____ How or why not?

4. Can you see God's protection from greater harm than the harm you received? _____ How or why not?

5. If you can see God's protection from greater harm, as expressed in question 4, please write a prayer of thanks to Him in the "Additional Notes" section on the following page.

ADDITIONAL NOTES

_____

_____

_____

_____

_____

_____

_____

_____

_____

_____

_____

_____

_____

_____

_____

_____

ISOLATED OR SET APART?

But the manifestation of the Spirit is given to each one for the profit of all: for to one is given the word of wisdom through the Spirit, to another the word of knowledge through the same Spirit, to another faith by the same Spirit, to another gifts of healings by the same Spirit, to another the working of miracles, to another prophecy, to another discerning of spirits, to another different kinds of tongues, to another the interpretation of tongues. But one and the same Spirit works all these things, distributing to each one individually as He wills. (1 Corinthians 12:7–11 NKJV)

1. Using a Bible dictionary, please write the definition for the word *sanctification* in the space below.
   Sanctification:

2. Please locate the following two passages in your Bible and write them in the spaces below.
   a. Romans 6:13:

   b. 2 Corinthians 4:6:

The word *sanctification* occurs thirteen times in the New Testament (Romans 1:4; 6:19, 22; 1 Corinthians 1:30; 2 Corinthians 7:1; 1 Thessalonians 3:13; 4:3, 4, 7; 2 Thessalonians 2:13; 1 Timothy 2:15; Hebrews 12:14; 1 Peter 1:2).

There are also seven topical verses in the New Testament, which are found in the gospel of John 17:17, 19; 1 Peter 1:2; 1 Thessalonians 4:3; 5:23; Hebrews 13:12; 2 Timothy 2:21.

I love the way *Easton's Bible Dictionary* describes sanctification. He states:

> Involves more than a mere moral reformation of character, brought about by the power of the truth: it is the work of the Holy Spirit bringing the whole nature more and more under the influences of the new gracious principles implanted in the soul in regeneration. In other words, sanctification is the carrying on to perfection the work begun in regeneration, and it extends to the whole man (Romans 6:13; 2 Corinthians 4:6; Colossians 3:10; 1 John 4:7; 1 Corinthians 6:19). It is the special office of the Holy Spirit in the plan of redemption to carry on this work (1 Corinthians 6:11; 2 Thessalonians 2:13). Faith is instrumental in securing sanctification, inasmuch as it (1)

secures union to Christ (Galatians 2:20), and (2) brings the believer into living contact with the truth, whereby he is led to yield obedience "to the commands, trembling at the threatenings, and embracing the promises of God for this life and that which is to come."

Being confident of this, that he who began a good work in you will carry it on to completion until the day of Christ Jesus. (Philippians 1:6 NIV)

The good work that began in you—in me—started when we declared with our mouths, "Jesus is Lord," and believed in our hearts that God raised Him from the dead (Romans 10:9). From this moment, we were justified in the eyes of God because of Christ's death on the cross and declared righteous because of our faith (Romans 4:5). The old man, our old nature, is now dead, and we were made new.

What does it look like to be made new? Each of us has different experiences when we accept our salvation in Jesus. Some people feel peace, joy, a sense of relief, and so on. For me, I felt as though I was freed from restraining jacket that was firmly wrapped around my soul. The moment I declared, "Jesus is Lord," with my mouth and believed in my heart that God had raised Him from the dead, I felt as though I was released from the bondage of my sin and could finally breathe easily. Because of my sin, I had reached a dark moment in my life. I was suffocating in despair and desperate for hope beyond measure.

The moment a person decides to follow Jesus, the Holy Spirit is sent to him or her and remains with that person forever (John 14:16–17). When the Holy Spirit comes, He does many things. A few of them follow:

- He becomes our advocate (John 16:7).
- He gives us life and power and develops the fruit of love, joy, peace, patience, kindness, goodness, faithfulness, gentleness, and self-control (Romans 8:10–11; 2 Timothy 1:7; Galatians 5:22–23).
- He corrects us when we are wrong and teaches us to do what is right (2 Timothy 3:16–17; John 16:8).
- He unites us with other believers (Acts 4:32).

- He distributes gifts/abilities to believers as He determines (1 Corinthians 12:7–11).
- He seals believers and is a deposit guaranteeing our inheritance until the redemption of those who are God's possession (Ephesians 1:13).
- He helps us in our weaknesses and intercedes for us in accordance with the will of God (Romans 8:26–27).

1. If you have confessed that Jesus is Lord, can you remember what your life was like before He came into your life? What is your life like now?

2. Do you find it easier to resist temptations that hindered you in the past or more difficult?

3. Are you aware of the role of the Holy Spirit in your life as a believer in Christ?

New Life in Christ

In a perfect world, I would tell you my life made a miraculous change, and I became a holy beacon of light for the kingdom of Christ. But my world was not so, and my thoughts and decisions were far from that reality as well. I would love to tell you all problems ceased to exist, and I had clarity about every decision that followed. But it was the opposite. The reality was that once I accepted my salvation in Jesus, the depravity of my sins were illuminated, and I realized how wrong I was in how I processed decisions. My old way of living life was no longer satisfactory in the eyes of God, and something in me would not allow me to remain the way I was. There was a new type of frustration stirring within me, one I found difficult to ignore.

Once I accepted my salvation in Jesus and was baptized, Kim and I moved, and my search for a home church began. After a short time of searching, I found one that I grew to love. I also met an amazing person, Bishop Woody. Bishop Woody eventually began to minister to me and guide me toward my God-given passions, which are prayer and serving in missions. He invested his time in teaching me how to pray according to God's will. He greatly supported me spiritually and financially in missions.

After a year or so, I started to notice the transformation God was doing in my mind and how He was reshaping my character. One day my heart had an aha moment, and the Word of God that was planted within me seemed to come alive. Nothing out of the ordinary was happening, but suddenly, I understood clearly and with certainty that my relationship with Kim was not correct in the eyes of God, and He was not willing to allow me to continue in that sin. A war had always been raging in my emotions, but this battle was very different. Even today I find it very difficult to find the words to describe it. All I knew was that I had a purpose, though I was not clear about what it was. But I knew my current situation was not a part of it. I began to withdraw emotionally from Kim and eventually moved into the other bedroom in our home. I was plagued by guilt and knew a decision had to be made. Kim had been very kind to me, but God was now the one I wanted to please. No one had ever ministered to me that my sin was wrong, but God did.

1. Can you think of a moment when you suddenly saw the reality of a circumstance you were in, and God was showing you it was time to deal with it? If so, what was it?

2. Did you deal with it the first time you became aware of it? If not, please explain how many times the thought kept returning to you and describe the intensity of each time it came to mind.

A Life Vest

> Woody Thomas, he was a very kind man. He invited me
> to start serving in their Tuesday night prayer ministry. I
> was clueless on how to pray. He taught me to take one call
> at a time and trust that God would give me the words to
> say. He later introduced me to missions. (from *A Shadow
> of Death*)

As I reflect on my relationship with Bishop Woody, I honestly believe he was operating in the gift of discernment when I was in his presence. I can remember catching his gaze in my direction. I thought it a little weird and figured him to be deep in thought of something other than what was happening in the moment. Today, I honestly believe he saw that spirit of homosexuality still operating in my life yet chose to look past it to see my heart and desire to worship and honor the Lord. I believe God gave him a heart of compassion toward me. I was still struggling with mentally breaking free from that lifestyle because it was something I had grown attached to. In my mind, the relationship was not simple to walk away from. I am a loyal person, and that was the main instrument used against my heart as I struggled with the decision to end it. Kim and her family had showed me great kindness. I am still grateful for how they treated me as one of their own. I was torn by the belief that I owed them a form of payment for how good they were to me. I also believed I had too much to lose and no vision for anything different. So yes, it was very frightening and caused me to experience fears of rejection, shame, and again loneliness, which is how I felt before meeting her. I never learned how to truly heal from the trauma that created those fears, so I learned how to substitute pleasures with the various types of sins with which I became involved.

It's funny how a war can be taking place within your heart, and the individuals who surround you daily are never fully aware of the true matters of your heart. I was plagued with a tremendous amount of weight from guilt because I was starting to feel unfaithful to God in my relationship, which I now had with Him. Why? Because I was now learning that my body is the temple of the Holy Spirit. According to the Word of God, there is no other relationship permitted for intimacy outside a union between a husband and wife (Hebrews 13:4; 1 Corinthians 7:2). And because I now had the Holy Spirit dwelling within me, I could no longer remain comfortable in this sin, which the Holy Spirit was confronting me with during that time.

1.   Has anyone ever suddenly come into your life who you are grateful for today, and your life is very different now because of that person? Who and how?

I was starting to drown in my weakness, but the Lord, in His mercy, provided a life vest for me through Bishop Woody. I say Bishop Woody was my life vest because God used him to reveal the source of my true passion, my true desire for life. God took away the ashes of something that was unholy and replaced it with something beautiful.

> But he said to me, "My grace is sufficient for you, for my power is made perfect in weakness." Therefore I will boast all the more gladly about my weaknesses, so that Christ's power may rest on me. That is why, for Christ's sake, I delight in weaknesses, in insults, in hardships, in persecutions, in difficulties. For when I am weak, then I am strong. (2 Corinthians 12:9–10 NIV)

I became more involved in church activities and developed a greater interest in the Word of God. My heart was now more focused outward, on others, rather than having a consuming concern about myself. I found my desires and priorities starting to adjust and shift toward what I believed God desired and prioritized. God's Word was proving to be true in my life. My inward transformation was being reflected outwardly through the renewal of my heart according to the Word of God. Praise the Lord for His goodness!

2. Who are you a life vest for today, or would you consider asking God to make you one for someone else?

> Therefore, I urge you, brothers and sisters, in view of God's mercy, to offer your bodies as a living sacrifice, holy and pleasing to God—this is your true and proper worship. Do not conform to the pattern of this world, but be transformed by the renewing of your mind. Then you will be able to test and approve what God's will is—his good, pleasing and perfect will. (Romans 12:1–2 NIV)

A Living Sacrifice

Many who knew me a few years before and observed the moment I was now in would stand as witnesses that God had done something radical in my life. For the first time, I felt like a had sight and was no longer under the shadow of death. A shadow that was killing my emotions, killing my dreams, and ultimately, killing my body. In God, I now had hope and learned how to dream again.

1. What are you grateful for today that God spared your life from in your past?

All the unhealthy passions I previously had were being poured into something holy and pure. Oh, how awesome and wonderful is the Lord God Almighty. I thank Him for meeting me where I was and not condemning me for my choices yet granting me knowledge and guiding me to make better ones. Lord, thank You for Your faithfulness, mercy, and grace. No longer was I concerned about what would happen to me, what I would lack, or what I would do without the support of another person. The fears of rejection from my childhood upbringing and the shame and abuse I experienced in past relationships no longer consumed me. I learned how to trust in Jesus during this difficult time in my life. I learned how to have faith and trust that He would take care of my needs and to trust in the plan He has for my life. Now was the time to walk closer with Him to discover that plan.

Bishop Woody passed on into glory with the Lord. I was blessed to say goodbye for now and promised him that I would see him on the other side. I have not met anyone since more precious to me than he was. Though I have gratitude for many wonderful men and women of God who have come in and gone out of my life, Bishop Woody is dearer to my heart because I experienced God's unconditional love when I was in the worse state I had ever been in my soul.

Extra Mile: Has God used a person to help you discover a greater purpose in Him, in your life? If not, write a prayer asking Him to provide one. If so, write a prayer of gratitude to God.

Forgiven Much

I cannot tell you exactly when the scales were removed and the light of His Word illuminated my lifestyle. The reflection I saw was that my heart knew it was not right. I shared what the Lord revealed to me to Kim, the woman I was in a relationship with, but unfortunately, it was not a mutual decision for us to go our separate ways. I soon moved out of the townhouse we were sharing and into a condominium of my own. I started to attend a new church because of its mission outreach ministries and became more involved in church ministry.

Funny, it seems like God's transformation of my life intensified after our separation. I am reminded of the story of Abram and Lot. God told Abram to go, but Lot went with him (Genesis 12:4). How I identify with this passage of scripture is; when God gives you instruction for your life, it often causes a type of loss—a loss of relationships, loss of a job, a home, or position in the community. The decision that causes the loss usually comes from a conscious decision made because of a change that is taking place within your heart. But if you decide not to walk away from relationships, a job, a home, or a position within your community, circumstances will begin to take shape, and various types of chaos and unrest will frequent your life. Your decision will finally come, but not in a peaceful transition. Rather, it will be a transition that creates more harm than necessary. Change is good but can easily become harmful when we do not accept the obvious time when it is necessary.

God instructed me to depart the relationship with Kim and draw closer to Him, He did not necessarily say others would be going with me into this new season of life into which he was preparing for me to venture. To this day, I am still very encouraged and hopeful when I read the story of Abraham, who was called Abram before God changed his name. Abraham was just an average man. The Bible does not indicate that he was born into a family of prestige; nor does it list any special skill sets, abilities, or educational background. Though later in life he was very wealthy and esteemed, he was born into a household of difficulties and its dysfunctions. Abraham's brother, Haran, died so his father adopted Haran's son, Lot. And Abraham's brother, Nahor, married his niece, Haran's daughter (Genesis 11:27–29). Abraham's ancestors were idol worshippers and did not honor the God of heaven as the only true God (Joshua 24:2). Yet God saw what Abraham could become instead of what he was. One could have a great understanding as to why he took Lot with him; his father, Terah, passed away while they were living in Harran, and Lot would have been left alone (Genesis 11:31–32). We all reach a point in life when we must decide if we want a relationship with God or live a life without Him. This was a defining moment for both Lot and Abraham. Both had reached a point in their lives when they would become solely responsible for their own choices and actions. Lot departed from Abraham (Genesis 13:5–8, 11). After a shedding of Abraham's past, God once again reminded him of the promise (Genesis 13:14).

I cannot claim ownership of the promise of Abraham to be mine, nor embrace it as God's plan for my life. Abraham's promise was unique for him, uniquely designed by God for the nation of Israel that would soon be birthed through Abraham. I identify with how God chose him and used him despite his past. Seeing this example in Abraham's life gives me hope for mine. Why? Because I know that God is no respecter of persons, and I trust that He was very intentional when He created me. It was time to separate from my past so God could teach me about my future.

1. What about you? Who in your life should you be separated from today?

2. Who in your life is preventing you from entering the unique promise God has spoken to your heart?

3. Is that person worth forfeiting your relationship with Almighty God? Please explain.

Extra Mile: If you are struggling to separate yourself from an unhealthy relationship, please write what those hindrances are on the "Additional Notes" page at the end of this section. Also, write a special prayer to the Lord and ask Him for the strength to choose His will over yours.

A Godly Sorrow

Godly sorrow brings repentance that leads to salvation and leaves no regret, but worldly sorrow brings death. (2 Corinthians 7:10 NIV)

If you are experiencing grief, sadness, or conviction right now, then you are in a good place. Honestly, I pray that you are. I pray that God grants you a godly sorrow so that He may transform your heart back into the beautiful masterpiece He created you to be. Please do not resist the discipline and pruning process. Trust me: The result of freedom in any area of brokenness is a savor of sweetness that cannot be explained.

What does a godly sorrow look like? It looks like what I am doing here—publicly sharing with you the sin that had me blinded to my identity in God. The sin that had me in bondage with Sam and deceived with Kim. I would not say that either of them were bad people. They were very beautiful as individuals, but when we became compatible through our fleshly desires, we all chose a path of destruction that would eventually end in death and eternal separation from God.

> Why do you see the speck that is in your brother's eye, but do not notice the log that is in your own eye? Or how can you say to your brother, "Let me take the speck out of your eye," when there is the log in your own eye? You hypocrite, first take the log out of your own eye, and then you will see clearly to take the speck out of your brother's eye. (Matthew 7:3–5 ESV)

Who am I to judge another person on their struggles, no matter what those struggles may be? Remember in the preface section of the book I said we would revisit the section in the Bible about the woman of sin who entered the room and washed Jesus's feet with her tears and then dried them with her hair? I greatly identify with her in many ways. I have lived a very sinful life. Many of my choices still haunt me, and I have much sorrow over them to this day. But I learned of Jesus, and I sought Him. I chose to believe that He was who I had heard He was. After discovering to the best of my ability that everything ever said about Him is true, I submit my life to Him daily to be sanctified of all the sin that still easily entangles me. I humble myself under His mighty hand of correction and allow Him to teach and instruct my days by the Holy Spirit. I often have encounters with individuals like Simon, who still pass judgment on me because of my past and because of the imperfections of my present. But Jesus has made it clear to me that I am His beloved, and I am forgiven in Him. Is it easy? Of course not. Is it worth it? Absolutely.

> A woman in that town who lived a sinful life learned that Jesus was eating at the Pharisee's house, so she came there with an alabaster jar of perfume. As she stood behind him at his feet weeping, she began to wet his feet with her tears. Then she wiped them with her hair, kissed them and poured perfume on them.

When the Pharisee who had invited him saw this, he said to himself, "If this man were a prophet, he would know who is touching him and what kind of woman she is—that she is a sinner."

Then he turned toward the woman and said to Simon, "Do you see this woman? I came into your house. You did not give me any water for my feet, but she wet my feet with her tears and wiped them with her hair. You did not give me a kiss, but this woman, from the time I entered, has not stopped kissing my feet. You did not put oil on my head, but she has poured perfume on my feet. Therefore, I tell you, her many sins have been forgiven—as her great love has shown. But whoever has been forgiven little loves little."

Then Jesus said to her, "Your sins are forgiven."

The other guests began to say among themselves, "Who is this who even forgives sins?"

Jesus said to the woman, "Your faith has saved you; go in peace." (Luke 7:37–39, 44–50 NIV)

Let us pray:

Heavenly Father, thank You for revealing to us the error in our ways. For every believer in the Lord Jesus Christ, You have provided the Holy Spirit as a counselor and comforter to guide us throughout life. Father, You are aware of the wars we have within ourselves that rage against Your plan for us. You said in Your Word that Your grace is sufficient for us, and Your power is made perfect in weaknesses (2 Corinthians 12:9). We pray for the power of Christ to rest upon us and strengthen us in our weaknesses. In Jesus's name, Amen.

QUESTIONS TO PONDER

1. How do you identify with the story of the woman we just read of in Luke 7 and why?

2. Have you ever been like Simon, passing judgment on someone else's sin? If so, please write a prayer of repentance in the "Additional Notes" section of this chapter.

3. Has God ever asked you to do something that would better your circumstances, but it could also cost you everything you learned to depend on? If yes, what was it?

4. How did your life change after you were obedient to His will or after you decided to reject His will?

5. Can you see God's patience and respect for you in making your own choice to choose His way or your way?

ADDITIONAL NOTES

_____

_____

_____

_____

_____

_____

_____

_____

_____

_____

_____

_____

_____

_____

_____

_____

_____

_____

FREEDOM AND RESTORATION

Therefore, there is now no condemnation for those who are in Christ Jesus, because through Christ Jesus the law of the Spirit who gives life has set you free from the law of sin and death. (Romans 8:1–2 NIV)

Using the English Standard Version of the Bible, please fill in the blanks for the passages below:

1. Matthew 26:28: "(Jesus said) For this is my _____ of the _____, which is _____ out for _____ for the _____ of _____."

2. Hebrews 10:17: Then he adds, "I will _____ their _____ and their _____ _____ no _____."

3. 1 John 1:9: "If we _____ our _____, he is _____ and _____ to _____ us our _____ and to _____ us from all _____."

4. Acts 3:19: "Repent therefore, and turn back, that your _____ may be _____ out."

I acknowledged my sin to you, and I did not cover my iniquity; I said, "I will confess my transgressions to the Lord," and you forgave the iniquity of my sin. Selah. (Psalm 32:5 ESV)

Deed and Truth

Now free from the past but intimidated by the future, I became aware of how so much was changing like I never imagined. The struggle to go through life on my own was very lonely and uncertain at times. The roots of rejection, shame, and abandonment had not been removed from my heart. I was left with many scars and in desperate need of healing. The defense system I developed over time was to silence the pain I experienced from them with physical desires. Now the alcohol was gone, the relationships were gone, past friendships were gone, and I was living in a state with no friends or family nearby. Now what? That was the big question. So I started pouring myself into ministry and found a reason to be in and around the church. I was afraid of what I was prone to do and did not yet trust myself to have too much idle time on my hands. I started down the trail of trying to please God by how much I could do for Him. There was so much that I still did not know about Him. Though my mind was being renewed from the old way of living life for Him, my knowledge of His character and how He loved me was very far from my understanding. I often swayed to the "broad path." What was the broad path? In this case, the broad path was substituting types of pleasures that were filling voids only God wanted to fill. But in my ignorance, I piled on the distractions, balancing several ministries at one time, attending a study group, and hosting a Bible study in my home. I had not learned that He was setting me apart to heal my soul and preparing me for His glory. I was afraid of silence and unused time, so I kept busy with church-involved activities.

> For it is by grace you have been saved, through faith—and this is not from yourselves, it is the gift of God—not by works, so that no one can boast. (Ephesians 2:8–9 NIV)

I still struggle to find the balance to understand these verses. As a single person with no children, shouldn't I be the first to show up to serve? Well, yes and no. You see, God looks at the heart. At that point in my life, I was still looking for approval from people, so I targeted my affection toward Him for the wrong reasons. The character of my nature had not changed; only the target of my affection was different. There is a way that seems right to humankind, but it eventually ends in death (Proverbs 14:12). How can pouring myself into the service of God bring death? Easy. When I go on a path that He has not ordained for me, I will not be able to rest in the completion of what He tasked me to do. If I serve Him on a mission trip to Albania but He is equipping me or has equipped me to serve the people group of Mexico, how is that a gain for His glory? Yes, people will be helped, but how many people would be negatively affected if I am somewhere He did not send me?

Let us consider a practical example. I have many years of experience in education. As an educator, I encountered various obstacles daily. I became skilled at managing temper tantrums, potty accidents followed by meltdowns, staff meetings and trainings, deadlines, weekly and daily planning, parent-teacher appointments, facilitating seasonal events and activities, ensuring each student is getting adequate attention for his or her needs, observing and understanding their individual needs, remaining flexible and on high alert at all times, going on a chase when little ones think you are playing a game but are chasing them to keep them safe from a danger they are not aware of, and so on. Or I could have had a mental breakdown under the pressure. I think you get my point. Let's say I have all the abilities mentioned above and honestly believe I can walk into a corporation and present my skill set for a completely different profession, like accounting. Yes, I am thorough, detail-oriented, and have many other skills that would be suitable for this position. But is this the best fit for me and my God-given passions that have already been made clear to me? Yes, I would be helpful and could probably become a great employee. But is this God's best for me and the institution based on the plans He has already established? There are many parts of the body for a reason. We all need each other to function properly. I pray that I am never in a place of ministry within the body of Christ where God has not directed me to be. I never want to be the one to make service for my Lord complicated because I am hindering progress or causing confusion.

Please take the time to read the book of Jonah.

One might ask, "Well, are there not places in scripture that speak about Christians doing good works?" Yes, there are. Several places in the New Testament speak on this topic. One of my favorite passages of scripture is found in Titus 2:11–14 (NLT):

> For the grace of God has been revealed, bringing salvation to all people. And we are instructed to turn from godless living and sinful pleasures. We should live in this evil world with wisdom, righteousness, and devotion to God, while we look forward with hope to that wonderful day when the glory of our great God and Savior, Jesus Christ, will be revealed. He gave his life to free us from every kind of sin, to cleanse us, and to make us his very own people, totally committed to doing good deeds.

Good deeds are the things God has equipped you for. How do we know what He has equipped us for? Seek Him to learn about the plan He has for your live.

When I started to pursue understanding Him and His plan for my life, I found myself lost. I had become a stranger to the person I once was. I have never had a problem with developing friendships or engaging in social activities. But during this season, I found it very difficult to talk with others and even more to connect with them. My life had been turned upside down, flipped inside out, and ripped into multiple pieces. The place in life in which I was then living was unfamiliar. I had no way of explaining what was happening inside my heart because I did not understand it enough to put it into words. The more I tried to explain my present state, the more frustrated I became. The frustration then caused me to struggle with rejection and shame all over again. So I decided to detach myself from others.

1. Have you ever felt misunderstood, and it caused you to retreat into isolation?

2. If so, did your decision to retreat help or cause you to feel more pain? Please explain.

3. Fill in the blanks using Hebrews 10:24–25 (NIV) as a guide. "And let us consider how we may _____ one another on toward _____ and _____ _____, not giving up _____ together, as some are in the habit of doing, but _____ one another—and all the more as you see the Day approaching."

4. After reading this passage, do you think isolation is God's will for you?

Loneliness in the Crowd

> Now the Lord is the Spirit, and where the Spirit of the Lord is,
> there is freedom. And we all, who with unveiled faces contemplate
> the Lord's glory, are being transformed into his image with ever-
> increasing glory, which comes from the Lord, who is the Spirit.
>
> Therefore, since through God's mercy we have this ministry, we
> do not lose heart. Rather, we have renounced secret and shameful
> ways; we do not use deception, nor do we distort the word of God.
> On the contrary, by setting forth the truth plainly we commend
> ourselves to everyone's conscience in the sight of God.
> (2 Corinthians 3:17–18; 4:1–2 NIV)

While I distracted myself with many activities, Bible studies, studying for the Bible studies, and church attendance, I started to notice that I still felt empty. The void was still there, even though I had filled all my free time with things concerning the Lord. By this time, I had established a healthy prayer life and spent consistent time daily studying the Word of God and writing in my journal prayers based on my daily reading. But somehow, I still felt empty, and loneliness consumed me. It was an emptiness that lingered and made its presence known. It would not go away; it wanted to be dealt with. So I did. I placed myself on a sabbatical. I spoke with my leaders and stepped down from all the ministries I was a part of. I handed off the Bible study that was meeting in my home to a person who attended. But I remained plugged in with the Bible study I was attending with a separate group of friends, and my church attendance on Wednesdays and Sundays remained the same. I placed myself in a season of waiting and observing.

Remember, I was still in the process of learning the ways of God and how often He shifts His dealings with us. I never knew there was so much about Him that my mind had not yet tapped. I was learning how big and vast He was, not only as my Lord, but during this season in my life, He was also becoming my Father and friend. Strange as it may seem, though I was listening and watching, I did not know what I was listening and watching for. I am naturally an observant person and quick to notice when patterns shift. There had been a major shift in my emotions, and something different was starting to take shape in my heart.

About a year and a half after I'd made my vow to the Lord, I was sitting in one of these presentations, and it happened: I felt that fire—the passion in me—as I had before. It was like my sight returned, and a cloud lifted. I could now see numerous possibilities, spanning beyond today and into many tomorrows. As I went further within the possibilities, it became too much for my mind to contain. I knew I was ready but was not yet given a direction. (from *A Shadow of Death*)

1. Can you recall a time when you became frustrated with the state of your life?

2. Why was that? Please explain.

3. What did you do about it? Why, or if nothing, why not?

4. Do you believe God placed that desire in your heart to change for the good?

5. Fill in the blanks using the NIV translation of the Bible:

   a. Nehemiah 7:5a: "So my God _____ _____ _____ my _____ to assemble the nobles."
   b. 2 Thessalonians 3:5: "May the Lord _____ your _____ into God's love and Christ's perseverance."

Guidance during the Waiting

I often reflect on that moment when the spark of passion for the Lord was reignited in my heart. It was during Missions Weekend at my church in Fort Lauderdale, Florida. During that time, progress updates were given on the various mission projects we were a part of as a church. Today I can see how God used that moment to reposition me for a very narrow path concerning my life. There was no greater joy than to experience the rush of hope flowing through my body. It was the greatest high I had ever experienced. It was like breathing in the fresh morning air on a spring day. My mind was clear and alert. The world around me seemed to be illuminated with colors so vibrant it was breathtaking to behold. But it was only for that moment. Yet that moment was so real that I can always—and to this day—go back to it and remember His faithfulness in lifting me out of the rut I found myself in. On remembering that moment in my life, I went back to the journals I'd kept. Some of the prayers and scriptures during that season follow:

- "don't take yourself too seriously—take God seriously." (Micah 6:8c MSG).
    - *My prayer*: Father, could You help me to not be legal in my walk with You? Help me to enjoy the journey.

- "But me, I'm not giving up. I'm sticking around to see what GOD will do. I'm waiting for God to make things right. I'm counting on God to listen to me." (Micah 7:7 MSG).
    - *My prayer then*: Father, hear my cry and lead me by Your righteousness.

- "Worship and recommit to God!" (Nahum 1:15b MSG)!
    - *My prayer then*: Father, I pray that Your grace covers me in this day. Continue to fill my life with Your presence. Continue to flow through my life for Your good.

- "In him we were also chosen, having been predestined according to the plan of him who works out everything in conformity with the purpose of his will, in order that we, who were the first to put our hope in Christ, might be for the praise of his glory." (Ephesians 1:11–12 NIV).

- ○ *My prayer then*: Father, I pray that You give me a clear understanding of Your will for me today, in Jesus's name, Amen.

I noticed several prayers of these types listed in the months leading up to the "spark." He was still leading me during the waiting, but I could not see it at the time. I became more anxious as the climax of the internal change continued. I was nervous and excited at the same time, but to my mind, I had no upcoming engagements that could cause my emotions to be as out of control as they were. I sought Him daily, and day after day, it seemed like there was no response. Only silence. But I continued to be faithful because that was all I knew to do at that time.

Suddenly, He responded by granting me renewed passion, and healing of the isolation I was feeling began. I had learned purposed isolation and how to intentionally be alone with God to study and search the Bible for daily guidance.

1. Have you ever found yourself becoming legalistic concerning your acts of service to God? If your answer is yes, please answer the following two questions.

2. How did God correct this action of legalism?

3. Write a prayer asking for forgiveness of the people you unknowingly harmed before God corrected you.

4. If you answered no to question 1, please write a prayer asking God to guard your heart against legalism.

The Invitation

It was an evening just like all the others. We gathered in the home of our leader, had a light snack, and fellowshipped with each other as our friends continued to gather. On this night, I was a little later than usual. On my arrival, I was a bit flustered because of my rush to get there before we began to worship. To my surprise, I arrived just before we all started to assemble in the living room and ready ourselves for worship and the teaching of God's Word. We worshipped together, and announcements were made as was the usual routine before starting our time of teaching. Once the announcements were finished, one of our friends was invited to share a part of her journey as a missionary there in Florida and what she felt God had next for her.

I had spoken with her on many occasions and even did some fieldwork with her downtown with our homeless friends. But she seemed different that night. As she shared her journey, I seemed to connect with her differently. Though I did not quite understand it then, she was the open door to the season God had in store for me. After she finished sharing her story, our leader came forward and gave an invitation. She was getting ready to move back home to Chihuahua, Mexico, and wanted to enter a season of rest to prepare for her next journey in Christ. Our leader gave the invitation for anyone who would be willing to help her with the process of moving home to her family and be open to helping her with anything else she needed throughout the process. We did not need to answer in the moment. He wanted us to take some time and pray to discover our roles in assisting her. He asked if we would email him before the next meeting what we felt the Lord was saying to us about how we could help her. The help could have been through prayer, financial assistance, or even escorting her back into her country and spending a few days helping her unpack and readjust.

When we met the following week, seventeen of us decided to come together as a group and accompany her home to her family. Many others contributed financially, and all of us committed to praying for the process.

We learned that a pastor and his family had moved to the city during her preparation time. They were sent there from one of our sister churches in Colorado to plant one in Chihuahua. Interesting coincidences started to unravel.

As a group, we communicated and coordinated plans to visit the pastor and his church to help with whatever needs they had, while assisting our friend in moving back to her family. We received clearance from our local church leadership team to go, and we were off to Mexico. While on the trip, we noticed quite a few projects that would require long-term assistance around the church and within the community. At one point, we started playing with the idea of an internship to help with their various needs. (from *A Shadow of Death*)

Through the group is how I found the path to Mexico. Was Mexico ready for me, or was I ready for Mexico? I guess only God's time will reveal this truth.

The two-week mission trip to help a friend turned into a six-month internship to help a church, which eventually turned into eight years maturing me in my faith.

"Hold your horses," you might say. "Where did a six-month internship come from? When was it decided, and how do you get eight years from six months? I thought you all were going to help a friend."

Well, that is what we thought too. The pastor of the church plant we served in Chihuahua and his team prayed about the idea, and we did as well. The final decision was left up to us. At the time, we did not know how many of us would return or who. While the seventeen of us were there on the trip, we would routinely have evening meetings before winding down for the night. During the day, we would be out in the community, serving the people with the church, or at the church working on various projects. Since there were so many of us, the church was able to divide us into smaller groups, which allowed an easier way for commuting throughout the city.

Those evening meetings were opportunities for us to share, pray, and give thanks to God for what He was doing there in the city. One night a leader expressed an impression that was placed upon his heart that there were two, maybe three of us from our group who would be returning for the internship that was previously discussed with the pastor. He said he was not sure who they were, but he knew it was a couple, maybe a few of us who was there in the room that night. Nothing more was said about the idea at the time.

On our last full day before the morning of our departure, we hiked up a small mountain. During worship and prayer, it was there that I knew in my heart I was one of the people who would return for the internship. I later spoke to my leader privately, and we began to pray about it independently. On our return to Fort Lauderdale, we had a debriefing meeting, and I later found out that two other people made the same decision I did. It was shared with the group the names of the three individuals who were returning to Mexico for the internship.

You cannot tell me that God does not have a sense of humor. He planted me in a foreign land where I could not initially speak the language. The closest people group to my skin tone were from Cuba, and I may have seen all five of them during my entire eight-year residence in Mexico. And when I did see them, they spoke a different form of Spanish, which meant I could not interact well with them either. Nothing was familiar. I had no crutch, and I was in a place where I was completely dependent on Jesus.

If I was going to survive, I needed to be willing to trust Him with all my heart, soul, mind, and strength. My path was very narrow, and I was in a perfect position to truly learn the depth of my love for the Lord.

QUESTIONS TO PONDER

1. Has God ever placed you among people who were very different from you, but your needs connected you?

2. Do you believe God was aware of your differences before He placed you in that group of people?

3. What does Proverbs 27:17 say? (Please write it in the spaces provided.)

4. What does the verse from Proverbs look like at work within the group of differences mentioned above?

5. Do you believe God is trying to work out a plan in your life?

6. Write James 1:2–4 in the space provided below.

Note: Look for how God brings these verses to life for you this week. Journal your experiences for encouragement in the days to come.

ADDITIONAL NOTES

BEAUTIFUL FEET

How beautiful on the mountains are the feet of those who bring good news, who proclaim peace, who bring good tidings, who proclaim salvation, who say to Zion, "Your God reigns!" (Isaiah 52:7 NIV)

Reflection Point

1. Let us take a moment and reflect on the past five years of your life. Are you able to see when God was working behind the scenes of your heartaches and the pain they caused?

2. Did you ever doubt that He was present with you? If so, why?

3. Please write verse John 14:18 (KJV) in the space below.

4. Did you find yourself avoiding communication with God during moments of sin or perceived failures of your past?

5. Please write the verse Hebrews 4:16 in the space below.

Reminiscing about His Goodness

As time quickly passed and the moments leading up to my departure for Mexico were now within a matter of a couple weeks, I reminisced about my time living in Fort Lauderdale. I am amazed at how God healed me in so many wonderful ways. I had arrived in Florida as a new believer in the faith, healed of some past hurts, but there were still many areas of my life that needed God's purification. I later went through a season of isolation, set apart for cleansing of past sins, brokenness, and harms done to me. My purpose was revealed to me when Bishop Woody later entered my life, and I later established many wonderful friendships based on acts of service within our community. Being a part of a group of Christians meeting in someone's home, a home group, is something I highly recommend because I was personally blessed by it in so many ways. I eventually learned how to have healthy friendships that did not involve wild partying, drinking, or intimate relationships outside the marital context. I learned how to love strangers. Many were closer to me than my family members.

The group I was a part of felt like a mini suburb of heaven. We were diverse in culture, ethnic backgrounds, and financial statuses. One person sold yachts for his father's company; another was a dishwasher in one of the local restaurants. What bound us together was our love for Jesus and our hearts for missions. It seemed like nothing of our personal lives mattered from the times we met for fellowship and ministry to the moment we departed from each other in anticipation of the following meeting. Our leader kept us connected electronically with short teachings, random jokes, praise reports, and present and future project updates during the weeks we were not together. We sometimes met for a sunrise worship service on the beaches of Fort Lauderdale and afterward, we would sometimes hang around for some beach volleyball. One of the girls from our group adopted a little boy, and we all came to her aid in support of necessities for the child and emotional support for her. Sometimes a few of us girls slept over at her place to help her adjust to the changes that came with becoming a single, full-time mother.

Another of our friends, a Caucasian woman with blonde hair and beautiful blue eyes later adopted two little African American girls with coarse, curly, dark hair. She was clueless about how to wash and maintain their hair. So a few of us took turns braiding their hair and teaching her how to do it until she eventually got the hang of it. Those moments are beautiful treasures that I still hold dear inside my heart. That home group was a beautiful blessing God used to show me His love. He affirmed me as an individual and showed me my value to His body of believers. In the act of pouring out of myself, I gained so much joy. It feels good knowing that the little you have and are willing to give away can add so much value to someone else's life.

1. Can you remember a time when you found yourself in a group of unlikely friends, and your life was significantly changed because of them? Good or bad, please explain.

2. How would your life be different today if you had never met them?

Purposeful Worship

A special moment I would hold dear to my heart for a lifetime is the ministry we did as a group. We called the activity "Love Bags." I do not remember how the activity began or who named it, but it was very fitting for what we were doing at the time. We filled ziplock bags with necessities and shared them and the love of Christ with the homeless. We regularly visited a few places in downtown Fort Lauderdale. We each brought something to the group: food, socks, toothbrushes, snack bars, small bottles of water, and so on. We combined the donations and evenly distributed them into extra-large ziplock bags, preparing as many as we could. There were special occasions when specific items were requested—like blankets, socks, and gloves—when the temperature was changing for the winter season. We included a simple preprinted message inside each bag: "Smile, Jesus Loves You."

We took the filled bags to our homeless friends and sat and chatted with them for a while. Sometimes our chats were spiritual in nature, about Jesus and His love. And other times, we had simple conversations about the weather. We were open to whatever our friends wanted to discuss. They were respectful because they had become familiar with our visiting times and began to anticipate our arrival. God richly blessed me through those relationships, and I cannot say that I have experienced a little piece of heaven such as that to this day. I am still fascinated at how different we were in our educational, financial, and social backgrounds, but we were so much the same when it came to Jesus. Only God can accomplish a beauty such as this.

I truly believe God used this group of friends to change my life. Like He used Bishop Woody to teach me how to pray and get me started in missions. This group of friends helped me develop purpose in my daily life while keeping God at the center of everything we did.

Therefore, the six-month internship was easy to grasp. It had become easy to give my life to something that I clearly saw as greater than any dream I previously had. I found it a great honor that God would choose me and grant me that opportunity to serve Him in that capacity.

1. Look up 1 John 3:16–18 in the ESV, and fill in the blanks: "By this we know _____, that he laid down his _____ for _____, and we ought to lay down our _____ for the _____. But if anyone has the world's goods and sees his _____ in _____, yet closes his _____ against him, how does God's _____ abide in him? Little children, let us not love in _____ or _____ but in _____ and in _____."

In preparing for Mexico, I think the people in our group ran faster with the vision than the three of us who were going for the internship. I am not sure if we were still in shock at what we were getting ready to do as interns or had full comprehension of the decision we had made to walk away from our lives for a short time. How can one truly prepare for an opportunity as great as the one God presented to us?

Many of my friends in other ministries I had served in or was still serving in would request one-on-one meetings with me. They would share very kind and encouraging words of wisdom, pray for me, and give me small gifts for my journey. I still have many of those gifts. They are a part of my precious treasures that I do not allow to be too far from me. One set of gifts I remember is from one of my dear friends from the choir. She served on an international mission trip before I met her, and she gave me her journals to learn of her story. When she would write to me, she would always call me "Pearl of Great Price." This name was something that I did not feel worthy of but later came to grasp the power in what that name reflects within my life. I will share a few more details relating to this topic in the following section. The church choir I was part of at the time, Calvary

Chapel in Fort Lauderdale, also prayed for me. Many of them continued to do so while I was in Mexico.

We held a Mexican-themed party as a fundraiser, and many people involved themselves in our support by donating their time, talent, energy, and finances. We had a live DJ, Mexican food, donations to be auctioned off, and handcrafted items. Some beautiful, hand-painted pieces of art were auctioned to help fund our upcoming trip. We invited a praise and worship dancer to come and minister to us with her gift of dance. Our leaders prayed a blessing over us, and we each got the chance to share a part of our testimonies and how we came to our decisions to intern in Mexico. God was and still is so faithful. It just blows my mind to know and experience His lavishness when you are in His will and heading in the direction He has determined for your life.

The house was so packed, inside and out, the front yard and the backyard. Because of all the activities that were going on, the home where we held the fundraiser was not able to carry the power wattages we were using. The breaker box kept tripping, leaving us in the dark a few times. But people from various churches kept coming, and they kept supporting. Most of them were our friends, but others were friends invited by our friends who wanted to provide support. It was a beautiful moment that I will treasure in my heart for a lifetime. Other than Bishop Woody, this was a memorable time I felt like someone believed in me and showed it through their involvement and support of various kinds.

2. Can you remember an occasion when God led you in a direction and unexpected support overwhelmed you? Please explain.

3. If you answered yes to question 2, in what ways did His provision increase your faith in what you were getting ready to do in His name?

Mission of the Heart

A few weeks passed, and we were off to embark on the six-month internship we had committed to. Sadly, I lost the first four months of the opportunity God had given me because of my preconceived expectations. The internship was nothing at all like the short-term trip we had taken months before. It was more intense and moved at a much slower and intentional pace than the mission trip. There was a lot of studying and planning involved. I would say 50 percent of our time was spent studying scripture, reading assigned books, writing/journaling activities, and doing personal research. Forty percent involved team service in and around the church and community; 9 percent of the time was spent in team-building activities. And 1 percent was personal time, though there was always someone in or near your presence. We ministered to the surrounding community, a group of children at an orphanage, and the staff and people of the church. Our situation was a bit tricky because we were still broken and needed to be ministered ourselves.

That 1 percent is what drove me insane. Until the internship, I had never been with someone or had someone constantly observing me throughout the day, seven days a week. In the beginning, it was madness. It was as though I was being smothered by an affection that was not known to me at the time. I did not understand what it meant for someone to care enough about me to invest his or her time into intentionally developing me for full-time ministry. My pride in entering that season of service for the Lord left me blinded by ignorance. I had finally discovered that my service in Mexico was not only for the people of Chihuahua, but it also served as great value for myself.

God was working out the plan He has for my life. At that time, His plan involved placing me in a foreign land, where I no longer had transportation of my own and could not clearly speak the language. My only option was to learn to trust in His care for me during that time. So He stripped me of my independence, my ability to run away from His discipline, and my ability to voice my dislike of the process because I could not effectively speak the language. When I became angry, by the time I figured out how to communicate my anger in words, I found myself more frustrated at the process itself, of trying to figure out how to communicate the incident that occurred. The problem no longer seemed important enough to even bother with. This was His brilliant way to teach me that sometimes, you must let things go.

I also learned how to choose my battles wisely and had a few Spanish phrases on hand to communicate my disagreement. Eventually, my Spanish words of choice had been cleaned up quite a bit and were now very appropriate to share in a church or around children. Trust me, the Lord was doing a very holy work, a mission within my heart through the friction that was taking place around me.

> Iron sharpens iron, and one man sharpens another. (Proverbs 27:17 NASB)

My personality is naturally very introverted, but I can be extroverted when there is an absolute need to be. I enjoy time alone with my thoughts to reflect on past experiences, to plan for current projects, and to strategize for their execution with excellence. Today I am learning how to control and balance that preference because God's desire is for us to learn how to thrive in a community of His people. I am learning that most of my isolation is a result of major insecurities that I have not properly dealt with. Nor was I ready or willing to confront them during my internship in Mexico. To be honest, my readiness is still not where it should be and is a present struggle in matching up with God's will for my life.

My prayer:

> Heavenly Father, grant me the strength to be vulnerable in Your sight and to trust in the love that You have for me. Heal me of all my emotional brokenness by the power of the Holy Spirit. In Jesus's name, Amen.

That was a simple prayer I prayed when I noticed my need for change. God introduced me to a recovery group that helped to set me on a track of progress. The progress I learned through this group set me on a path of deeper and intentional sanctification in Jesus. Lord willing, I will discuss the process in more detail in an upcoming book.

1. Has your natural personality type or preferences ever clashed with God's will for your present season of life? If yes, what was the experience like?

2. Have you learned, or are you learning, how to allow God to mold you into His will for your life? Please explain what the process was/is like.

Around the fourth month of my internship, I became humble enough to see that I still had a great deal of transformation to succumb to and that I did not have ministry figured out. I exalted my knowledge above those who were responsible for me because, in my mind, I was there to serve them in their need. And I was completely ignorant of my own deep-rooted needs. Through much heartache, frustration, and fits of anger, I eventually accepted the pruning and disciplining God chose for my life at that time. My responsibility was to also find rest in His design, which was reshaping my character for the season to come.

By the time the end of the internship rolled around, I had learned many skills, ranging from simple construction and plumbing and crafts. I even learned how to work the soundboard and recordings for the women's ministry. I learned how to study the scripture more in-depth, managed several translation projects, worked on administrative projects, and learned cleaning techniques. And I learned how to live based on a biblical worldview. What is a biblical worldview? A biblical worldview is the lens through which you view the world based on the Bible, God's Word. I learned how to make better decisions in finances, how to respond respectfully to leadership, how to put a filter on some of the words I spoke, and how to be cautious of my actions and responses based on what the Bible has to say about them. To make a quick note, none of them were perfected. Instead, I realized how far from perfection I was.

The value of patience was discovered in serving the people of the city until they were able to grasp an understanding of how to run the ministry God had sent us to establish for them. I still have immense gratitude to the people of Chihuahua for their patience with our process, their service to us in helping us navigate the city, their help in developing our Spanish-speaking skills, and the wisdom of what they taught us regarding common dangers to foreigners in the city. I am grateful to the staff members who chose to set aside a portion of their time to love on us through our brokenness as we discovered a greater intimacy in Christ Jesus, our Lord.

Once the six-month internship ended, I decided to renew my commitment to continue to serve the church in Chihuahua for another year, but financial support was only covered and committed to through the initial six months. One couple continued to support me for many years, but I still had to make some tough choices and had a sit-down with my heavenly Father to come up with a plan. The support from the couple was not sufficient to cover my monthly living expenses, which meant I would not be able to remain in full-time ministry.

After several weeks of prayer, God's plan started to take shape at a rapid pace. A one-to-one ESL (English as a second language) teaching opportunity came to me, which turned into a three-year job teaching kindergarten. The young woman I was teaching the one-to-one classes to was the English coordinator of a reputable school there in the city. She decided to take English classes to sharpen her English skills and later recommended me to her director for the position that needed to be filled as their kindergarten English teacher.

I clearly remember my first day of class. I was very numb to my emotions and tried to convince myself that this would not be hard at all. I convinced myself it would be just like the classes held at the orphanage. I did not consider the daily schedule that needed to be adhered to and the responsibility of the curriculum and the daily planning. By the way, how do you keep five- and six-year-olds calm when you cannot speak their language and they cannot speak yours? The assistant they assigned to me in the classroom could not speak English either.

Reality was quickly setting in. I remember standing in front of twenty-three curious faces intensely staring at me as I froze with a blank look of horror on my face. So what do you do? I immediately thought, *Children like to play, and I like music. Let us incorporate the two.* I was hoping it would buy me some time to formulate a plan. The song "Hokey Pokey" became my all-time favorite. This brilliant idea, which definitely came from God, worked, and all of us survived the day. By God's grace, I managed to keep the job, and they even helped me navigate the process of obtaining a residency visa within the country. They allowed me time during my work schedule for required meetings with their immigration department. My manager at the time attended those meetings with me to translate and help me fill out the required documents.

After three years of teaching kindergarten, I accepted a one-year teaching opportunity at a Christian elementary school teaching ten- and eleven-year-olds. From there I was recruited by a parent of one of my students. His father was the human resources manager at the top aviation company in the country, and I was invited to spearhead an English-teaching pilot program in their organization. My reach with them spread across six of their seven plants. God set me before their top engineers and all their managers and department heads. They were all very aware of my mission work in their city, and my Lord used my life mightily for His glory among them. This organization, Textron Aviation, even helped me with and contributed to my permanent residency visa status in Mexico. They were very kind to me, and I made every attempt to show them my gratitude through the quality of work I produced for them. My employment came with permission from my church leaders, and my service to the church did not change. My ministry projects eventually became more evening- and weekend-focused.

The skills I learned during those eight years I could never credit to my abilities. I never studied for anything I was able to accomplish during my time in Mexico. I look at my accomplishment of successfully developing, launching, and leading my kindergarteners through a spelling bee in which the competition was so fierce, they had to stop the event because we ran out of words. The course that was built with my hands and included an online platform dreamed up by me and which I managed. I can only give glory to God for these wonderful successes. The results produced through these accomplishments added value to everyone involved. An accomplishment that will last a lifetime has the potential to reproduce achievements thereafter. Only a Holy God can produce experiences such as these through a broken and sinful person such as I was and am.

> Brothers and sisters, think of what you were when you were called. Not many of you were wise by human standards; not many were influential; not many were of noble birth. But God chose the foolish things of the world to shame the wise; God chose the weak things of the world to shame the strong. God chose the lowly things of this world and the despised things—and the things that are not—to nullify the things that are, so that no one may boast before him. It is because of him that you are in Christ Jesus, who has become for us wisdom from God—that is, our righteousness, holiness, and redemption. Therefore, as it is written: "Let the one who boasts boast in the Lord." (1 Corinthians 1: 26–31 NIV)

QUESTIONS TO PONDER

1. How do you feel about conflict? Why?

2. Fill in the blanks below using Matthew 18:15–17 (NIV) as a guide.

    "If your brother or sister _____, go and point out their _____, just between the two of you. If they _____ to you, you have won them over. But if they _____ not _____, take one or two others along, so that 'every _____ may be _____ by the testimony of two or three witnesses.' If they still _____ to listen, _____ it to the church; and if they _____ to listen even to the _____, treat them as you would a pagan or a tax collector."

3. Do you practice this section of scripture? Why or why not?

4. Do you ever feel the strong urge to isolate from friends or family members?

5. If so, have you ever asked God to show you why you feel the need to do so?

ADDITIONAL NOTES

_____

_____

_____

_____

_____

_____

_____

_____

_____

_____

_____

_____

_____

_____

_____

_____

_____

_____

PEARL OF GREAT PRICE

Again, the kingdom of heaven is like a merchant looking for fine pearls. When he found one of great value, he went away and sold everything he had and bought it. (Matthew 13:45–46 NIV)

Remember the missionary friend I mention in the previous section, stating that she always called me Pearl of Great Price? My curiosity eventually led me to research the formation of the pearl, which I found very fascinating. They have always been very beautiful objects to behold, but I never understood the rigorous process they experience in being formed. They are formed in clams or oysters, where their homes are found in the deepest depths of the ocean floor. Clams and oysters feed off all types of garbage that sinks there. Though they are scavengers, they can produce the pearl, which, to some, are worth a great price in monetary standards.

The formation of the pearl occurs when the clam or oyster opens its valve to feed, which causes the mantle to be exposed. Exposed to what? A grain of sand, the egg of a parasite, or even a parasite itself. All are common in the aquatic environment. As the irritant becomes lodged in the mantle, the oyster or clam instinctively produces thin layer after layer of nacre around the irritant to avoid further harm. And during this process, the pearl begins to form.

> If you declare with your mouth, "Jesus is Lord," and
> believe in your heart that God raised him from the dead,
> you will be saved. (Romans 10:9 NIV)

As a believer in Christ Jesus, our pearls of great price begin to form the moment we declare with our mouths that Jesus is Lord and believe in our hearts that God raised Him from the dead. Throughout our lives, there are various irritants surrounding us in our living environments and have been since the day we were born. Adult influence, the friendships we allowed into our lives, the choices we made because of our present understanding or lack of understanding we held, those irritants began to form and produce various sinful habits some of us still practice.

1. What irritant, sin were you exposed to in the past that has produced a harmful habit in your life today?

2. How are you instinctively covering your sin to minimize the harm being done to yourself or others?

Rigorous Formations

Because we are broken vessels, we encounter various irritants each day. They include lust, anger, fornication, thievery, deceit, and judgement. Our mantle, in this example, are our souls, the emotional parts of our beings. These irritants have a way of teaching us characteristics that contradict the character God desires of us.

> The acts of the flesh are obvious: sexual immorality, impurity and debauchery; idolatry and witchcraft; hatred, discord, jealousy, fits of rage, selfish ambition, dissensions, factions and envy; drunkenness, orgies, and the like. I warn you, as I did before, that those who live like this will not inherit the kingdom of God.
>
> But the fruit of the Spirit is love, joy, peace, forbearance, kindness, goodness, faithfulness, gentleness and self-control. Against such things there is no law. Those who belong to Christ Jesus have crucified the flesh with its passions and desires. Since we live by the Spirit, let us keep in step with the Spirit. Let us not become conceited, provoking and envying each other. (Galatians 5:19–26 NIV)

How do we develop the characteristics of the Spirit, the characteristics of love, joy, peace, forbearance, kindness, goodness, faithfulness, gentleness, and self-control? Isn't it something that should happen once we have given Jesus Lordship over our lives? That would be a perfect world, and all of us would be living in a state of complete bliss and harmony. If you are a Christian or know one, you are able to testify that this is not the case. Though we have been spiritually born again, we must now learn how to live according to the plan and intentions God predesigned for our lives.

However, though there is a plan and predesign for our lives, we still have free will to accept or reject God's best, what He desires for us. So again, how do we develop the characteristics of the Spirit? By living one day at a time and forming a discipline of obedience. Just as the oyster is not able to drive out the irritant, we are not able to drive out our sinful tendencies. It is only through the grace of God that we can overcome brokenness in Christ Jesus with the leading and guidance of the Holy Spirit. In Jesus, the blood from His sinless sacrifice on the cross covers our sins and makes us right before God. Through the Word of God we are sanctified by the truth (John 17:17), which is what Jesus prayed to the Father for us to obtain. Once we allow our lives to become encapsulated into Christ and remain there, it prevents further harm from being created. It is there in this sacred place that our pearls of great price begin to form and take shape. So does life become perfect, and we start to live each day victoriously? Of course not. We are scarred emotional beings, and the journey of our sanctification into holiness will continue until the day Christ returns or calls us home.

> But he was pierced for our transgressions, he was crushed for our iniquities; the punishment that brought us peace was on him, and by his wounds we are healed. (Isaiah 53:5 NIV)

Unjustly punished, Jesus allowed Himself to be wounded for our transgressions (sins). He voluntarily took them upon Himself, which provided a way of reconciliation for us with God the Father. "The punishment that brought us peace was on Him," was the due justice we owed God, which Jesus freely paid for. "By His wounds we are healed," provided salvation from our sins and all their eternal effects.

For God to start revealing the treasure He placed in me, this opportunity to serve Him in Mexico was the tool He used to open my eyes to understanding. I discovered how to see God beyond the surface of the obstacles.

Pearl of Great Price, you are free in Christ Jesus. Choose this day to accept that freedom you have received through His sacrifice.

1. Using Matthew 5:16 (NIV), fill in the following blanks: "In the same way, _____ your _____ _____ before others, _____ _____ may _____ your _____ _____ and _____ your _____ in _____."

2. Have you ever experienced hostility from those who love you when you try to live out your freedom in Christ? Please explain.

3. How does this make you feel?

4. Because of the actions of the people who love you, do you withdraw from the love of Christ (His guidance), or do you press more into His instruction for your life?

5. For either action noted in question 4, how does this make you feel? For example, if you withdraw, do you feel regret, sadness, and so on? Or if you press more into Him, do you feel isolation, misunderstood, and so on?

6. Write a personal prayer to God or for strength in the "Additional Notes" section on the following pages.

Trusting with a Broken Heart

> Have I not commanded you? Be strong and courageous. Do
> not be afraid; do not be discouraged, for the Lord your God
> will be with you wherever you go. (Joshua 1:9 ESV)

Joshua 1:9 was spoken to Joshua after Moses passed away. Moses was used mightily as a vessel to reveal God's strength to the tyrannical leader of Egypt. After many harsh demonstrations of God's power, the Israelites were finally freed from Egypt but had not yet entered the Promised Land before Moses died. Joshua was chosen to lead them into the land, and God provided him clear instructions on what he was to do regarding the direction He was getting ready to lead them. I would imagine encouragement was a definite need for Joshua, as it would soon be for me.

Six years had passed, and the mission of the church plant was finally fulfilled. Throughout the years, other interns and missionaries would come and support the work we were doing in Chihuahua. The pastor of the church and his family decided it was time to return to their home in Colorado. He formally announced the new senior pastor and supporting pastors of the church. All of us, the missionaries and other interns, were removed from leadership. New leadership was established, chosen from the people of the community who had been under our guidance over the years. I remember our last meeting together as if it were yesterday. I asked him if this was an "Exodus," and if it was time for me to leave as well. He said no. "You should only leave when God tells you where to go, and until then, stay planted where you are." So I was obedient and remained planted.

> And you divided the sea before them, so that they went
> through the midst of the sea on dry land, and you cast
> their pursuers into the depths, as a stone into mighty
> waters. By a pillar of cloud you led them in the day, and
> by a pillar of fire in the night to light for them the way in
> which they should go. (Nehemiah 9:11–12 ESV)

I am sure each of us who served on that church plant in Chihuahua experienced many transformational moments as we laid down our plans for our lives there. Many opportunities were opened to us to share the gospel as the Lord held back resisting forces that attempted to prevent us from doing so. I had become more sensitive to the guidance of the Holy Spirit by His leading during ministry and leading for the sake of obvious safety precautions. I know I had many failures, but I know God accomplished more successes through my failures. Some of my poor choices I will never recover from, some I am in the process of recovery, and others I have already been restored. Praise God for His mercy! My faith was tremendously developed in the Lord because of that experience, and our relationship has become more intimate.

Two years later, after the original senior pastor and most of the team had departed, I was soon approaching my eight-year anniversary of service. I noticed my heart toward the people of the church and community was becoming noticeably different. I started to become frequently fatigued, and my level of patience with the culture had significantly changed. So one day during my devotional time with the Lord, I asked Him if it was time for me to return home. In my mind, home was Fort Lauderdale, Florida. Florida is where my soul came alive in Him and my purpose was discovered. Chihuahua was where I gained opportunities to practice all that He was developing within me. The process was intense, invasive, and at times, very confrontational. I learned how to depend on others and how to function as a family. I discovered new passions and many beautiful things that God salvaged and made new in my life. Through many mistakes, I learned how to hope and listen more. I am so grateful He did not allow me to give up on the process or allow me to quit.

For the individuals who were chosen to be my leadership team, I thank God for their lives to this day. No, it was not always easy to accept their direction or receive their constructive guidance. In fact, I rejected it often, and my heart understood it at the time as a form of rejection. But the seeds of loving correction were planted, and God eventually yielded an increase. I praise God for granting them His patience and love to guide me closer to His purpose, even when I could not follow the leadership He placed in my life with grace and humility.

> Whoever heeds life-giving correction will be at home among the wise. (Proverbs 15:31 NIV)

1. Can you think of anyone God has used to help you through a difficult time in your life? Write their name(s) in the space below.

2. If you wrote a name below question 1, did you find it easy or difficult to receive their constructive guidance? Why or why not?

3. What did you learn while being led by them?

4. If any, please list any regrets you may have from that time of discipleship.

5. Write a prayer of thanksgiving and a prayer of blessing over their life (lives) to God for their service to you during that season of your life.

6. If you at first rejected their guidance, write a prayer to God of repentance for rejecting His hand of correction during that season of your life.

After a time of struggle within my heart, I decided to talk with one of my pastors from the church there in Chihuahua. I shared with him how anxious and irritable I had become and that I no longer felt a sense of contentment. I expressed that I was not sure if the time had come for me to leave. My heart was so torn. Thinking back, I believe I already knew the will of God for that season of my life, but I was choosing ignorance, to remaining in disobedience. In a sense, I was looking for a leader to agree with my decision to remain disobedient. Yet again, this is a beautiful reflection of a living God. He loves us too much to not allow intentional or unintentional rebellion to separate us from His love. God was leading me to make the conscious decision to obey Him. My leader advised me to put a time frame on it, pray about it, and set it aside. And when I revisit it again at the end of this time frame, see what the Lord has to say about it. I took him up on the challenge.

I set aside a few days praying about my heart and decided to leave the idea alone for ninety days. During this time, I resisted the urge to dwell on the thoughts about this decision until the time frame had ended. Once it was finished, I still felt unclear about the direction God was giving. So I took the question back to my leaders and asked if they could pray with me as well. After a time of prayer, we all reached the same conclusion. It was time for me to return to my country, but not to Florida. It was to Texas instead.

Everything in my fervor wanted to resist this direction, but my heart would not allow me to. God had made His will clear to me through His Word, through prayer, and through leadership for this upcoming season of my life. I found myself very afraid of the transition. Why? Because I knew I was a very different person than I was when I left my hometown as a teenager and living the entirety of my adult life away from home. Not only did I not know how to live among my family, but my childhood friends as well. You see, when I left Texas, Jesus was the furthest thing from my mind. Yes, church attendance was a given, but I was far from having an intentional relationship with Him, and the choices of my life were far from a biblical worldview. I humbly laid down my will and accepted His. I chose to trust Him even with a broken heart.

7. Have you ever received direction from the Lord that you were not ready to accept? If so, what was it?

8. *Note*: The following questions should only be answered if you answered yes to question 1. Why were you finding it difficult to accept?

9. What were the results once you did, or what were the consequences when you did not obey the Lord's direction?

10. Do you have any regrets of your delay in responding to Him or your decision not to respond to Him?

Kicking against the Goad

Please set aside some time to read Acts 23–26 for the complete context of the following section.

I am reminded of the story of the apostle Paul and his conversion to being a follower of Christ. Strong disagreements would often break out after he shared the truth about Jesus. In this case, some Jews from the Province of Asia disagreed with how Paul was ministering and decided to stir up a commotion (Acts 21:27–28). After much chaos, Jesus stood near Paul and said, "Take courage: As you have testified about Me in Jerusalem, so you must also testify in Rome" (Acts 23:11 NIV).

Paul was then transferred to Caesarea, where he stood before the governor Felix (Acts 24:1–2) and left in prison for two years. At the end of Felix's term, he was succeeded by Porcius Festus. Three days after arriving in the province, Festus, the new governor, went up from Caesarea to Jerusalem. The chief priests and the Jewish leaders appeared before him and presented the charges against Paul (Acts 25:1–2). They wanted him transferred to Jerusalem from Caesarea and have him killed along the way (verse 3). Festus discussed Paul's case with King Agrippa because he was at a loss on how to investigate the matter (Acts 25:13–20).

King Agrippa wanted to hear from Paul himself (Acts 25:22), so Paul was presented the opportunity to share his testimony before the king. What stands out to me most about Paul's testimony is when he shared what Jesus stated to him in Acts 26:14b: "It is hard for you to kick against the goads."

Like many of us, I am sure there are times when Jesus has tried to get our attention or guide us in a better direction because of the plan He has for our lives. But we made the choice to not adhere to His guidance. So what do we tend to do? We kick against the goad.

What on earth is a goad, and what does it look like? The outline of biblical usage describes it as, "an iron goad for urging on oxen, horses and other beasts of burden, hence the proverb, 'to kick against the goad,' i.e., to offer vain and perilous or ruinous resistance." The transliteration of the word is "kentron". Goad was a common expression in Greek and Latin literature. It looks like a long stick with a pointed end and is sometimes called a cattle prod.

Reality was evident. It was time for me to hand off God's treasure that He allowed me to help build and maintain. I sensed an immense testing of my heart. I struggled to resist selfishness and control. It was evident that there was still the root of arrogance within my heart, but fortunately, I had grown in maturity to where I was more pliable in the hands of a mighty God. So as He continued to prod me in the direction of my family in Texas, I moved quickly, without hesitation. I gave no room for the mental gymnastics that I tend to take myself through. Nor did I provide a place for the enemy to cause me to question the will of God.

My quick response was to not allow sin of the heart or dark spiritual influences to plant seeds of doubt against the known will of Jesus for that moment in my life. I gave myself a deadline of thirty days. Within those thirty days, I resigned as an employee of Textron Aviation, paid off any open accounts, which included the purchase of a car. The church of Chihuahua prayed for me, and I said my goodbyes to the friends I made during my time of residence there. I partook of the painful bitterness of leaving what I learned to love and cherish to the sweetness of taking up my cross and following Jesus into this next season of my life in Him.

> Then he said to them all: "Whoever wants to be my disciple must deny themselves and take up their cross daily and follow me. (Luke 9:23 NIV)

105

QUESTIONS TO PONDER

1. Please fill in the blanks for Proverbs 3:5 using the NIV translation:
   "_____ in the _____ with all _____
   _____ and _____ not on _____
   own _____."

2. What is your definition of trust?

3. Using the *Online Merriam Webster Dictionary*, fill in the blanks to complete the definitions of the transitive verb tense of the word *trust*.

   a. "To _____ on the _____ or _____ of: Believe
      i. To place _____ in: _____ on a friend you can trust
      ii. To _____ or _____ _____ trusts that the problem _____ _____ resolved soon"
   b. "To _____ or _____ in one's _____ or _____: Entrust
      i. To permit to stay or go or to do something _____ _____ or _____
      ii. To _____ _____to"

4. How often do you evaluate your trust in the Lord Jesus?

5. Has there ever been a moment when you leaned on your own understanding and the outcome was not what you expected? If so, please explain.

ADDITIONAL NOTES

RESILIENT TRUST

This is the confidence we have in approaching God: that if we ask anything according to his will, he hears us. (1 John 5:14 NIV)

Home in Texas and still on fire for the Lord. But my blaze was soon quenched when I was struck with the sudden blow of my new reality. Everything I learned in Mexico, my spiritual foundations established, and my rebirth into Jesus through water baptism, was now all coming together to reveal the evidence of what Christ had accomplished within my heart. This new reality would now be to simply live life among family, old friends, and new friendships as well. Sounds simple, right? The truth is that this phase of life would prove to be more challenging than the ones previously experienced.

> Consider it pure joy, my brothers and sisters, whenever you face trials of many kinds, because you know that the testing of your faith produces perseverance. Let perseverance finish its work so that you may be mature and complete, not lacking anything. If any of you lacks wisdom, you should ask God, who gives generously to all without finding fault, and it will be given to you. (James 1:2–5 NIV)

My life was no longer prioritized by service in ministry. It was no longer structured with a daily agenda that included errands and reporting progress to others. My time had now become quite the opposite. There was no one holding me accountable, no one overseeing my progress, no one to serve. I soon started to feel a sense of uselessness and inadequacy.

The days seemed longer, my world was much smaller, and my vision of tomorrow was now extremely bleak. My mind, character, and priorities seemed broader than the territory where God had placed me, and I desperately needed Him to show me how to use what I learned within the new land where He had placed me. When thinking back on those initial days, months, and first two, I find it interesting that I never asked God for wisdom. Yet when I prayed, I asked many questions, complained, and resisted the new life He was trying to produce within me. I later noticed a trend. I easily adapt when I have understanding, but blind faith is what He requires of me. It is funny how our expectations naturally guide us in directions God never instructed us to go, but we expect Him to bless our efforts.

There is a way which seems right to a person. (Proverbs 14:12a NASB)

1. Has there ever been a drastic change in your life (good or bad), and you found yourself uncomfortably vulnerable to the change?

2. If so, what was it, and how did you initially respond?

3. Looking back on that experience with the wisdom you have today, how would you have responded differently?

Mission Shift

Somehow, I had it in my mind that life would magically fall into place, and God would immediately open doors of opportunity for me. Why? Because I am more holy, of course. Why would He not? I have laid down my life for Him for eight years, and my wisdom is now more profound of His truth. Or so I thought. I was quickly starting to observe how unholy I still was and realizing the obvious sanctification that still needed to take place within my heart. My little friend "pride" was still lurking about, and humility was desperately needed. It was obvious that my maturity in Jesus was far from complete.

> Likewise, the Spirit also helps in our weaknesses. For we do not know what we should pray for as we ought, but the Spirit Himself makes intercession for us with groanings which cannot be uttered. (Romans 8:26 NKJV)

Extremely stressed and aware of insecurity starting to surface anew, I was being challenged to see work and daily life as ministry and to approach it with a biblical worldview. So much had changed, and it was not only what was happening within me. Before my service of ministry in Chihuahua, employment was always easy to obtain. But this was no longer the case. I had been out of the country for eight years and intentionally limited my awareness of what was happening in US society. I did not follow social media much and was not very involved in the politics taking place during the eight years I was away from my country. Those actions were strongly advised to help our focus remain where we were planted during that time. When I returned in 2017, almost everything had gone electronic. Even applying for a job was now done online and rarely face-to-face, so I was forced to learn how to navigate my way through online employment search engines. The way of presenting yourself to a potential employer had also changed significantly from business professional to quite casual, which was very different from the way I was previously taught. I was raised with southern conservative mannerisms, and now it seemed a respectful, "Yes ma'am/sir," or, "No sir/ma'am," was no longer necessary. A résumé went from a one-page summary of employment to a mini-novel including a photo of yourself. I found myself in complete culture shock. I felt more like a stranger in my own country than I did living in Mexico.

The couple who supported me during the years in Chihuahua were married during those years. They were young adults, in their twenties and quickly gave birth to three small girls. A few months after my return to Texas, I learned of the husband's passing on into eternity, and my dear friend was now a young widow. I was not financially able to attend the funeral services and found myself in a state of grief that was seriously close to depression. The shock of my current situation was so profound that I did not have the words to seek God to understand why this was happening to me or even how to ask Him for guidance. I found myself learning how to live again through a new state of brokenness.

1. Have you ever been so deeply broken that you were at a loss for words before the Lord?

2. Can you remember if you still felt His presence with you? Describe this moment in the space below.

3. What did you learn from that experience?

Greater Value Than a Raven

> Consider the ravens, that they neither sow nor reap; they
> have no storeroom nor barn, and yet God feeds them;
> how much more valuable you are than the birds!
> (Luke 12:24 NASB)

According to a Barna Group research release in a *Culture and Media* article (April 28, 2012) on global poverty, "there is an estimated 1.4 billion people in countries outside the US who do not have access to clean water, enough food, sufficient clothing and shelter, or basic medicine like antibiotics." Not many of us here in the Western world would call this success or living an abundant life.

When we hear that God has a plan for our lives, what does that plan look like? Was this God's plan for the lives of the 1.4 billion individuals who were a part of the Barna Group research? Is His plan for our lives wrapped up in luxuries and bank accounts that have no end? What did Jesus mean when He said, "The poor you will always have with you, and you can help them any time you want" (Mark 14:7a)?

A part of my spiritual growth involved attending churches with various teaching styles. Some of them taught that if you have the faith to believe and confess with your mouth, you will obtain what you declare. I believe this kind of teaching mostly surrounds the following verses.

In John 14:12–14 (NIV), Jesus said, "Very truly I tell you, whoever believes in me will do the works I have been doing, and they will do even greater things than these, because I am going to the Father. *And I will do whatever you ask in my name, so that the Father may be glorified in the Son. You may ask me for anything in my name, and I will do it.*

The first part of the verse seems to be straightforward, but I found myself conflicted with the second part when Jesus says, "And I will do whatever you ask in my name, so that the Father may be glorified in the Son. You may ask Me for anything in My name, and I will do it."

That is a broad statement. Today I can, somewhat, understand where the "name it and claim it" movement came about among certain Christian congregants. Reading over this section of scripture, without proper context, it does sound like Jesus was implying we could bring the Father our shopping list of desires, and He would grant them to us as would a genie in a magic bottle. I believe this is the difference between religion and a relationship with God the Father through the Son. I cannot find anywhere in the scripture during the time of Jesus's ministry where He taught the crowds or His disciples to seek after worldly things. In fact, in Matthew 6:33, He specifically instructs the people to "seek first the Kingdom of God and His righteousness." I believe Jesus was more concerned about the ultimate resting place of the soul rather than the temporal state of the person here on earth.

1. What is your interpretation of John 14:13–14?

2. What do you think Jesus meant when He said, "seek ye first the Kingdom of God and His righteousness," in Matthew 6:33 (ESV)?

3. What did Jesus mean when He said, "the poor you will always have with you," in Mark 14:7a?

Kingdom-Focused

Please read Matthew 6:25–34.

Consider a relationship with a sibling, parent, or spouse. As the relationship progresses, you learn the other person's tendencies and responses to various topics and situations. You learn what the individual will and will not invest his or her time, energy, and finances. Throughout this learning, you gain understanding as to why the person will not participate in a thought, activity, or venture. As a parent, knowing the love you have for your child, I am sure you would like to give him or her the world. But you are also aware of the possible dangers if you were to do so. These dangers include not developing the skills necessary for and the value of hard work to obtain desired goals. Nor would they benefit from deciding the most cost-effective way to obtain the goals. So no, you would sometimes choose to hold back the wishes of your child to protect him or her from a harm or danger that, because of limited knowledge, the child cannot foresee.

Those who are married, I am sure you love your mates and would like to give them their hearts' desires. But there are always priorities, and sometimes the answer must be no, at least for the time being, depending on circumstances and future priorities for your family. As a friend, I have been able to express my love for my friends with a firm no simply because I loved them. How is this? For example, in that moment, my no to loaning them finances was not to harm them but to not enable them in their bad habits. Or my no to having another conversation about a topic that we have already discussed numerous times, and they are still not considering the advice I gave them.

What have we done in the previous scenarios? We have provided a broader view and shared the wisdom we have learned so the individuals, who we dearly love, might gain an understanding why a decision is not the best for them at this time—or possibly not in the future. I believe it is the same way when it comes to our relationship with our Lord.

I am not against financial wealth by any means. God takes great delight when we learn how to prosper financially. We can see many scriptural examples in the lives of Abraham, Isaac, Jacob, David, Solomon, and Job.

God even transformed an orphan girl and made her queen of a nation; read the book of Esther. He transformed the life of a pagan widow, who later accepted Him as God, and set her in the path of a wealthy kinsman redeemer; read the book of Ruth. But even in these examples, their wealth or social status (as in the case of Esther) was used for God's greater purpose. My view of this topic favors the means that God will choose to use for His will to be accomplished in this life. In my opinion, success in any aspect is not for our glory but to be used for the glory of God in this world that many would know that He is the true and living God. This same God is as engaged in every aspect of our lives as we allow Him to be.

The Voice of the Martyrs is a Christian organization I have followed for many years. They serve in countries like Ethiopia and seem to be concerned about getting basic necessities—like soap, undergarments, and toothbrushes—to people driven from their homes because of their Christian faith. Consider our Christian brothers and sisters in Afghanistan who need food, shelter, and Bibles. Or what about the Christians of India, who are radically opposed because of their faith? In September 2020, eighty-four of them were driven from their home in Chhattisgarh state. Last, but not the least, what about the Christians of Uganda, whose homes and land were taken away from them because of their faith in Jesus?

1. Please fill in the blanks below using Luke 22:39–44 (NIV) as a guide: "Jesus went out as usual to the Mount of Olives, and his disciples followed him. On reaching the place, he said to them, '_____ that you will not fall into temptation.' He '_____ about a stone's throw beyond them, _____ '_____ and '_____, 'Father, if _____ are _____, take this cup from me; '_____ not _____ _____, but _____ be '_____ .' An angel from heaven appeared to him and strengthened him. And being in anguish, he '_____ more _____, and his sweat was like drops of blood falling to the ground."

2. In Jesus's prayer above, whose *will* was answered?

3. What would life be like today if God had answered Jesus's prayer?

4. Please fill in the blanks using Matthew 6:9–10 (NIV) as a guide. "This, then, is how you should pray: 'Our Father in heaven, hallowed be _____ _____, _____ _____ come, _____ _____ be done, on earth as it is in heaven.'"

5. Have you ever had a deep desire for something and truly believed it was the will of God, but His hand never released that prayer request to you? What was your response, and why did you respond that way?

As our relationship develops in Christ, we learn of His ways, and our desires eventually become His desires. Observing how He cares for me and how He ministers to me in that given moment, I can make wise decisions as to what I would bring before the Father in His name. I learn to align my will with the will of Jesus. I learn to ask myself the following questions:

- Is my request glorifying God and how He can use it? Please read Isaiah 42:8 and Acts 12:21–23.
- Is my request in accordance with God's will? Please read 1 John 5:14; Matthew 6:9–10; 2 Peter 3:9.
- What is my heart's true motive? Please read James 4:2b–3.

What did this detour of information have to do with my move to Texas? Everything. My will was to return to Florida, but God's plans for my life trumps any plans I may ever have for myself. When I chose to make Jesus Lord of my life, a part of that meant that He would direct and guide me according to the plan God originally decided for me. Will I always understand His plans? Of course not. Will I learn to trust His will and develop faith in the things that are not seen? I truly believe it is possible to do so, over time and with a lot of obedience.

> "Before I formed you in the womb I knew you, before you were born I set you apart; (Jeremiah 1:5a NIV)

Slow and Steady

> I started a new job and found a home church. I lived with my mother for six months and then moved into my own home. The apartment I found was very humble, but I understood that this was a phase of repositioning, and I was sure that I was where God wanted me to be. (from *A Shadow of Death*)

Quite a bit of time passed, and stability was finally being found. Friendships were more challenging because my priorities were now very different. I now sought individuals who put into practice the biblical worldview that I had learned to live by. But my heart still longed for Mexico and Florida because of the friendships that were formed there.

I feel there were many times when I was being tempted to return to my old way of life. But I was too different now and found it impossible to be content with my previous worldview. God was so gracious toward me, and I had noticed that His leading and presence always remained the same. I was gradually learning how to apply what I discovered in Him over the past years to my present situations of life. I eventually learned that my mission field was now my place of employment and the community He placed me in. The same way I felt accountable to my leadership and the people of Chihuahua, I was now learning to feel toward the people God was bringing along my path here in Texas.

What were the differences between my service then, as a missionary in a foreign land, and now, being on a daily mission in Jesus? There was only one. I had become fully aware that God was constantly observing my actions and correcting my behaviors along the way. I have always been on a daily mission for Jesus. My perspective was in need of change. Without realizing it, I had tried to categorize my relationship with God based on locations and circumstances. I gradually started to realize this mindset was part of my biblical worldview as well. My prayer life strengthened and became more focused on how I could improve my witness of Him through my words and attitude. Especially when it seemed that I was the only one doing what's right according to the Word of God and now seem to be in the minority.

> And do not be conformed to this world, but be transformed by the renewing of your mind, that you may prove what *is* that good and acceptable and perfect will of God. (Romans 12:2 NKJV)

QUESTIONS TO PONDER

1. Do you live your life placing God first, your priorities first, or the priorities of your family first? Why?

2. If your friends and family members were asked to share their opinions about your relationship with God, what do you think they would say about you?

3. In the space provided, please write the verse for Romans 12:2.

4. Would you say your life reflects the daily mindful actions of Romans 12:2? Why or why not?

ADDITIONAL NOTES

_____

_____

_____

_____

_____

_____

_____

_____

_____

_____

_____

_____

_____

_____

_____

_____

_____

_____

PURGE THROUGH SANCTIFICATION

In a large house there are articles not only of gold and silver, but also of wood and clay; some are for special purposes and some for common use. Those who cleanse themselves from the latter will be instruments for special purposes, made holy, useful to the Master and prepared to do any good work. (2 Timothy 2:20–21 NIV)

From the time I returned to Texas, my life seemed significantly unstable. Each struggle was very different from what I had previously encountered, and some were new to me. One of the greatest challenges came when I became unemployed and found myself dependent on government assistance. This was a crushing experience for me emotionally and revealed additional pride within my heart. I had always been on the giving end of blessings and now realized I needed to learn how to receive. I later learned how God used that season of need to purge more of the pride from my heart. After about six months, I found another place of employment. God was amazingly faithful in providing for my monthly expenses, and I was able to continue to serve others out of my resource of time.

Another difficulty I encountered a few years after returning to Texas was when I was hospitalized for a period of two and a half months.

> The Lord makes firm the steps of the one who delights
> in him; though he may stumble, he will not fall, for the
> Lord upholds him with his hand. (Psalm 37:23–24 NIV)

God is very much in the particulars of every aspect of our lives. As I explained in a little more detail in my previous book, *A Shadow of Death*, I never had a desire to have roommates. Why run the risk of moving in with other individuals during a pandemic? But this door of opportunity presented itself to me mid-2020, while COVID-19 greatly affected the world. It appeared no one had answers, and it was not clear who to listen to during that time. Society, as we all knew it, came to a swift halt. What was more fearful and shocking to me was that churches were also closed without a biblical explanation as to why. Who could ever imagine a situation such as this? How do you function and still advance for the kingdom of Christ when you were not properly equipped to manage a season of isolation from everyone you love? I quickly learned of many individuals suffering from depression and experiencing various types of abuse. Many fell prone to alcoholism or went hungry because of the lack of employment. For the first time, the church was not available to support the weak and vulnerable. I am grateful that I was able to connect with other members from the church, and we began a weekly fellowship via Zoom to support and encourage each other.

The impression continued to grow within my heart to have a roommate for a short season. I was still unsure why I was sensing this need. The feeling was not because of the isolation; I did not mind that at all. Yet I strongly sensed the urge to do so. Early May 2020 an opportunity presented itself, and I made the transition to move out of my one-bedroom and into a three-bedroom apartment with two friends who attended my church. I'm glad I responded to the promptings of God. Late August 2020 I became very ill and had to be placed in ICU for a couple of months.

> On Saturday morning, August 29, I took a turn for the worse. At this point, I could not properly shower, clean my room, or make it to the kitchen for food because of my exhaustion. When I accomplished a task as simple as going to the bathroom, I gave thanks to God that I had made it. I shared a bathroom with Patricia, one of my two roommates. One day, she needed to use the bathroom, but I didn't have the strength to clean myself and get back to my room. Finally, after about thirty minutes of her knocking on the bathroom door and asking when I'd be finished, I cleaned myself up as best I could, got dressed, and went back to my room. When Patricia saw me in that state, she decided to take me to the emergency room. Her bedroom was next to mine, and she'd heard me, night after night, coughing—uncontrollably at times—and often asked if I was OK. I always said yes, even though I was not.
>
> I asked Patricia to pack a few of my things, and then she helped me out of the chair in my room and walked me to her car. She already had called around to the hospitals, looking for one that accepted my insurance, and she found one in Katy, Texas, roughly twenty minutes from our apartment. When we arrived, she got a wheelchair for me and helped me into the emergency room.
>
> Strangely, this was when I felt the most helpless. I submitted to whatever was going on within me. It seemed like my body knew it was in a place of safety and that

help was on the way. The last thing I remember was a nurse assisting me to intake. Patricia couldn't stay with me because of the COVID restrictions, but I believe God used her to save my life.

I tried to give the nurse my address, but my thoughts started to scramble. I later found out that I lost consciousness and collapsed during the intake process. The next thing I knew, as I slowly opened my eyes, I was in a different area of the hospital, in a smaller room. I was lying on a bed in the center of the room, surrounded by various machines. I had IV tubes coming out of my arms and a nasal cannula in my nose, providing oxygen, which they forbade me to remove.

I later learned that I had septic shock, double pneumonia, and respiratory failure, among other things. Both my lungs were covered completely with bacteria, in bad shape, and not functioning properly on their own. I kept running a fever, and I dreaded the cooling blanket they had me lie on to keep my body temperature down. My oxygen levels dropped for no apparent reason, and every time I coughed, my heart rate would soar. At one point, my heart rate was up to one hundred and seventy beats per minute.

Oxygen was only circulating through the top half of my body. They would switch me from a nasal cannula to a CPAP (continuous positive airway pressure) machine. They suggested placing me on a ventilator, but I rejected that option; I wanted the natural breath that God gave to me, not the breath created by mankind. Little did I know that the type of oxygen produced by human hands was from wisdom granted to them by Almighty God. Later, I flatlined twice, and my mother made the decision for them to place me on the ventilator. And what do you know, the man-made oxygen sustained me while my lungs healed. Praise the Lord for all His wonderful works! (from *A Shadow of Death*)

If I had not yielded to the guidance of the Holy Spirit to move in with roommates, only God knows what the outcome would have been. We were still in a pandemic, travel was limited, and my family lived in a different town. I was alone, and who would have known that my health was declining? God in His mercy had a plan.

> Trust in the Lord with all your heart and lean not on your
> own understanding; in all your ways submit to him, and
> he will make your paths straight. (Proverbs 3:5–6 NIV)

1. Has there ever been a moment when you felt the leading of the Lord in a direction that seemed to make no sense at the time?

2. What was it, and what were the results?

3. Do you ever wonder what life would look like today if you chose not to listen to the leading of the Spirit?

4. Do you believe that God has a plan for your life?

Better Days Are Coming

A few months before my hospitalization took place, I shared a dream with my sister. I dreamed of driving my car through a dense, wooded area on an unpaved dirt road. My car was filled with my personal items, leaving just enough space for me to drive comfortably. As I neared the end of the road exiting the forest, the path ended on an old and rugged low-lying bridge.

The boards of the bridge were badly worn, reflecting natural deterioration. The riverbed beneath it was now dried out and overgrown with green brush. I also noticed how still and peaceful the environment was surrounding me. There were no movements, no wind, and no sounds that you would naturally hear in a forest. There was another road just ahead of me, and I could only turn left or right. I remember processing the decision within myself on which way I should go. My attention took a sudden shift just off the path toward a subtle sound that broke the silence. I glanced in my left sideview mirror and noticed a piece of the bridge, to the left of my rear tire, had been broken a bit, revealing a bird nesting just beneath it. Frightened because of my disturbance, it hopped out of its nest and ran into the crossing road. I stepped out of my car and frantically went after the animal. As I approached the road before me, I gained more visibility and could see deep curves on both ends. The bird and I were positioned between two spots blind to other travelers. I remember thinking, *O Lord, what if a car comes around the curve and causes harm to this creature.* I felt myself frantically trying to figure out how to get it back to safety and protect the bird from injury without causing harm to myself as well. You'll be happy to know that the rescue effort was a success, and I was able to get the animal and place it back safely into its nest. Not a single vehicle had passed down the road.

I got back in my car and observed how perfect the view before me was. The trees were lush and green, the road was freshly paved, and the rays of the sunlight were very inviting to the senses. You could still see a light misty dew hovering between the trees as they were ruffled by the light breeze. I felt a sense of newness and found myself very refreshed as I awoke from that dream state.

A month after I was discharged from rehabilitation, I learned to walk, talk, eat, and care for myself again. I sought the assistance of a realtor to help me find an apartment to rent because I was still not too familiar with the city. After sharing my preferences with her, I she said, "I know of this perfect little place that I think you will be really happy with." I took her at her word and drove over to see it. I agreed to the terms of the lease, and the move-in date was set.

At that time, my sister still lived a couple hours away from me, so she and her husband drove over to help out with the move into my new apartment a week after I signed the lease. I was still unsettled about the monthly rent and a bit scarred by the difficult financial season I experienced eighteen months earlier. I was afraid of the commitment. But with the support and encouragement of my sister and her husband, I went forward with the plan to move into the apartment. After all, the lease was already signed.

Very early in the morning of my move, I found myself driving along a winding road with lush trees on both sides. I stopped by the apartment to drop off a few boxes and clothes that were inside my car and headed back into town to meet my sister and her husband to go for a rental truck to move my furniture from storage into my new place. My car windows were down, and there were no other cars on the road. The only sound I could hear was the wind blowing as I traveled along the road. The morning dew hovering between the trees captured my attention. The scene instantly triggered the memory of the dream I had months prior. A great joy came over me. I picked up the phone, called my sister, and reminded her of the dream I shared with her months before. She was not far from me and said excitedly, "Chris I see seven planes flying over the area in perfect V-shaped formation!" I knew in my heart, in that very moment, that I was where God desired me to be for this season in my life.

> Take delight in the Lord, and he will give you the desires of your heart. Commit your way to the Lord; trust in him and he will do this: He will make your righteous reward shine like the dawn, your vindication like the noonday sun. (Psalm 37:4–6 NIV)

1. Have you ever experienced the fear of starting over after a difficult moment in your life or the life of a loved one?

2. Describe your fears during that moment in the space below. If more space is needed, please use the space on the "Additional Notes" page at the end of this section.

3. Using the Bible verses of John 16:13–15 (NIV), please fill in the following blanks: "But when _____, the _____ of _____ , comes, _____ will _____ you into _____ the _____ . _____ will not _____ on _____ own; _____ will _____ only what he _____, and _____ will _____ you what is _____ to _____. He will _____ _____ because it is from _____ that _____ will _____ what _____ will make _____ to _____. All that belongs to the Father is _____. That is why I said the _____ will receive from _____ what _____ will make _____ to _____."

4. Looking back on that fear you experienced, can you see how the Spirit of truth guided you through that difficult moment.

5. Today, will you choose to trust Jesus more with your life? Why or why not?

A Time of Refreshing

The move was a success, and I absolutely fell in love with the place. As I remind you, God is into the details of our lives. It's a rather large apartment complex, but how my building is positioned, it feels much smaller than it really is. The community is secluded, surrounded by lush trees. A state forest is within walking distance. Yet there is a major highway only three miles away. The surrounding neighborhood is filled with various amenities for the family and shops to perform the necessary daily errands. I marveled at the height of the ceilings, crown moldings, appliances, and even a narrow view of a wooded area, perfectly positioned across from my bedroom and living room window. It's as though the apartment was designed and built specifically for me. I truly feel refreshed, and He is making all things new.

I will refresh the weary and satisfy the faint. (Jeremiah
31:25 NIV)

Over time, I entered a new season in Him with more opportunities
of maturity. As I reflect over the years of my walk with God in Christ
since1999, He has truly been faithful. God has delivered me from the
addiction of alcohol and healed me of some insecurities and dependencies
I had on others. Rejection does not control me to the degree that it once
did. I am now able to see moments of rejection as opportunities for God
to eventually provide for me His best. I can see His care for me in real
time, daily. I am no longer imprisoned by the humiliation from people or
situations of my past because God used these experiences to strengthen my
confidence and trust in Him. And has affirmed me as His child (Romans
8:16), who He has fearfully and wonderfully made (Psalm 139:14).

My intrigue now draws me deeper into my relationship with God. I
am aware of how He is renewing my mind and teaching me a better way
of thinking and viewing life and the challenges that come with it. I have
learned that I will have good days and bad ones, but He has promised that
He will never leave me nor forsake me (Hebrews 13:4–6). I trust that the
trials God allows into my life have a specific purpose to mature me (James
1:4; Romans 5:3–5), to correct me of my sinful choices (Hebrews 12:6; Job
5:17; Psalm 94:12; 2 Timothy 3:16), or to direct me toward His highest
good for my life (Psalm 23:2–3, Proverbs 3:6; 4:18; Isaiah 26:7).

Glorify the Lord with me; let us exalt his name together.
(Psalm 34:3 NKJV)

"Well, now what?" you may ask. The journey of sanctification continues
until Jesus calls us home to be with Him or when we are raptured if you
are a Christian. He grants us comfort in ensuring His return for us in the
following verses:

And if I go and prepare a place for you, I will come again
and receive you to Myself; that where I am, there you may
be also. (John 14:3 NKJV)

> But of that day and hour no one knows, not even the angels of heaven, but My Father only … Watch therefore, for you do not know what hour your Lord is coming. (Matthew 24:35, 42 NKJV)

> Do business till I come. (Luke 19:13b NKJV)

When Jesus returns for me, I want to be found a good steward over the business of the things concerning my life over which He has granted me stewardship. I want to be found faithful of using the abilities He has blessed me with in bringing glory to the kingdom of heaven. I want to be found faithful in the stewardship over how I invest the time that He has rewarded me with here on this earth and use it to advance His kingdom. I want to be found faithful and hear those words, "Well done, good servant" (Luke 19:17).

QUESTIONS TO PONDER

1. What is in your life today that God has revealed to you in the past?

2. Christian, God has revealed a future to you in John 14:3 and Matthew 24:35, 42. He said, "The Son of Man (Jesus) will come at an hour when you do not expect Him." When Jesus comes for you, where will He take you?

3. Do you believe God's plan for your life is about the life you are living or the life that is to come?

4. How are you preparing for that day, the day of Jesus's return?

5. If He returned today, will you be found a faithful steward of the business of your life? Will you be found a good and faithful servant?

ADDITIONAL NOTES

THE COMMISSION

And Jesus came and spoke to them, saying, "All authority has been given to Me in heaven and on earth. Go therefore and make disciples of all the nations, baptizing them in the name of the Father and of the Son and of the Holy Spirit, teaching them to observe all things that I have commanded you; and lo, I am with you always, even to the end of the age." Amen. (Matthew 28:18–20 NKJV)

What is the business Christ has given you to do until He returns or calls you home to be with Him? The business He has for you—or your life's mission—could be easier to focus on if it is crafted into a statement of mission. Businesses devise mission statements and are managed within the guidelines of those missions. A mission statement for a business states the aims or values a company or organization is governed by. Your life has a mission, and you should make a daily statement so it will be governed by something. The question is: What will you allow to govern your life? A mission statement filters out unfruitful relationships and places of employment, hobbies that prove to be a waste of time, or activities that are a waste of finances. Your mission statement should sum up who you are and who you desire to become.

When considering a mission statement or statement of mission for my life, I considered all the passions in my heart. I reflected on what God has revealed to me in times of prayer and reflection on His Word as I saw myself being a vessel to be used to accomplish the things He has granted me the abilities to do. I considered the things that I am naturally good at and how I could use them to bless others. Finally, I factored in what I need to do to continue to enhance them, which will keep me in constant devotion with Jesus for guidance.

I eventually came up with my mission statement/statement of mission:

> As a Christ-follower, my daily aims are to love the Lord my God with all my heart, soul, mind, and strength. In Jesus, I face life's challenges, go where He sends me, and love others as I love myself through various acts of service. This is how I daily take up my cross. My life is committed to making disciples, which includes a commitment to teaching them how to obey everything that Jesus has commanded me. As I keep watch for His return, I will continue striving to become more like Jesus through prayer and daily devotion in the Word of God by the power of the Holy Spirit.

Those who are closest to me can attest that I make every effort to live my life according to my mission statement. Am I perfect? Do I often feel like I have greatly disappointed my heavenly Father? Do I struggle to forgive? Do I struggle with selfish sin? Does my mind wonder away from the truth of God's Holy Word? The answer is yes to all those questions. If I had reached perfection, I would not be in constant need of a Savior. Through dying to my desires and passions daily and embracing the desires and passions of Jesus, my sanctification makes me holy and more like Him, which is the will of the Father.

Beloved, you were chosen, and God has a plan for your life. He paid a great price for you by sending His only Son, Jesus, to die on a cross. And He was raised from the dead that you may have fellowship with Him. Jesus's desire for you is that your eyes are opened and that you turn from darkness to light, and from the power of Satan to God so that you may receive forgiveness of sins and a place among those who are sanctified by faith in Him (Acts 26:18, revised).

The purpose of your life is that you are conformed into the image of Christ through a process of sanctification. For God did not call us to be impure but to live a pure and holy life (1 Thessalonians 4:7). Sanctification is continuous. To be transformed into Christ's image, your passions, habits, and thoughts eventually become more like His. Can these things be done in your own strength? No. Only God is able to make these changes take place within you, and He does it by the power of the Holy Spirit. How is this made possible? Please read John 15:4.

What is your purpose? What has Jesus commanded you to do until He returns for you? Please write out the scriptures in the spaces below:

Mark 12:29–31

Matthew 28:18–20

Matthew 24:42

On the "Additional Notes" page that follows, write your own mission statement using the scriptures you just wrote as a guide. Make a commitment to daily live out your mission statement by the power of the Holy Spirit from this day going forth.

Final Encouragement

As Jesus humbled Himself even to the point of death, we must humble ourselves daily in the hand of a good and loving God. I pray that the testimony of my life through this book has challenged you to pursue Christ passionately. I pray that you were able to see past me, the individual, and were able to see God's consistency throughout these parts of my journey of hope. I pray that you have gained a deeper knowledge and awareness that He has a plan for your life. I pray that you are aware that your life has purpose. And may the God of hope transform your passions, thoughts, and every intention to become more like Him each day as you trust that He is with you every moment of every day. May you know Him deeper as He continues to reveal His love to you. In Jesus's name, Amen.

> May God himself, the God of peace, sanctify you through and through. May your whole spirit, soul and body be kept blameless at the coming of our Lord Jesus Christ. (1 Thessalonians 5:23 NIV)

ADDITIONAL NOTES

_____

_____

_____

_____

_____

_____

_____

_____

_____

_____

_____

_____

_____

_____

_____

REFERENCES

Topical. "Sanctification." Bible Hub. Accessed September 4, 2022. https://biblehub.com/topical/s/sanctification.htm.

Thayer's Greek Lexicon, Strongs G2759. "Kentron." Blue Letter Bible. Accessed May 23, 2023. https://www.blueletterbible.org/lexicon/g2759/niv/mgnt/0-1/.

New Choices Treatment Centers Admin. "Using the Jellinek Curve to Chart a Path to Addiction Recovery." New Choices Treatment Centers. Accessed January 7, 2021. https://newchoicestc.com/blog/using-the-jellinek-curve-to-chart-a-path-to-addiction-recovery-nc/.

Redwine, Elliott. "What Are the Stages of Alcoholism?." Peace Valley Recovery. Accessed July 5, 2022. https://www.peacevalleyrecovery.com/blog/what-are-the-stages-of-alcoholism/.

Ingram Content Group UK Ltd.
Milton Keynes UK
UKHW012105170723
425314UK00013B/208/J